LEARNING SCIENCE
PROCESS SKILLS

LEARNING SCIENCE PROCESS SKILLS

Second Edition

H. James Funk

Associate Professor of Education
Indiana University at South Bend

Ronald L. Fiel

Professor of Science Education
Morehead State University

James R. Okey

Professor of Science Education
University of Georgia

Harold H. Jaus

Associate Professor of Science Education
Purdue University

Constance Stewart Sprague

Adjunct Faculty for Indiana University
South Bend

Kendall/Hunt
Publishing Company
Dubuque, Iowa

Cover photo: © James L. Shaffer

Copyright © 1979, 1985 by Kendall/Hunt Publishing Company

ISBN 0-8403-3510-5

Printed in the United States of America
10 9 8 7 6 5

The authors wish to acknowledge and give thanks to Cincy Borne and Michelle Funk who contributed to this text by providing many of the drawings used as illustrations.

CONTENTS

PREFACE

To the Reader:

If you want to make science in your classroom more interesting, more than recalling facts, this book is written for you. Whether you are a seasoned veteran or neophyte, LEARNING SCIENCE PROCESS SKILLS will help you develop the knowledge and skills necessary to bring science process skills to the classroom.

What are science process skills? They are the things scientists do when they study and investigate. Science process skills are the vehicle for generating content and a means by which concepts are formed. Whether your students learn (or will learn) science from a science kit, textbook, or both, these skills are something your students ought to learn. It will help them in science, other subjects, and, more importantly, life.

This book is presented in three parts. Part 1—Learning Basic Process Skills attends to the kinds of science skills appropriate for preschool and the lower elementary grades. In Part 1, you will learn and practice observation, communication, inference, measurement (metric, of course), classification, and prediction. In these early chapters you will learn the skills through activities selected from exemplary elementary science programs. In Part 2—Learning Integrated Science Process Skills, you will learn more complex (integrated) skills, the same kinds of skills older children should possess. In Part 2 you will learn the kinds of things scientists do when they plan and conduct controlled scientific investigations. Part 3—Content . . . Process . . . Concepts and the Nitty Gritty of the Classroom provides some valuable guides to help you teach the facts and concepts of science through the process skills. Part 3 also identifies several valuable science resources and, like Parts 1 and 2, contains activities and ideas for your classroom.

The text is designed to enable you to learn at your own pace. Each chapter begins by identifying the objectives you will achieve by doing the activities that follow. As you proceed through the structured activities, you will be given directions and asked to write responses to questions. Self-checks are given so you can monitor your progress. At the end of each chapter, you can take a mastery test so you can determine your level of proficiency with the material.

One more word about this text . . . With every adventure there lies a risk. The risk here may be one of oversimplification. In truth the processes of science are interdependent. As you study the processes, however, it is hoped that the somewhat artificial separations created here will dissolve and you will become more aware of the interdependency of the processes involved in doing science.

The Authors

INTRODUCTION

There are several possible approaches to the teaching of science to elementary school children. One approach is to emphasize the *facts* of science. Another is to teach the *concepts* developed by science. And, finally, one may teach the *processes* through which science uncovers facts and develops models.

Science teaching that uses a *factual* approach is primarily concerned with imparting the findings of science to students. The end of instruction would be the student's acquisition of the following type of information:

A hydrogen atom has one electron.
Mercury is the planet closest to the sun.
Snakes are reptiles.
Water freezes at 0°C.

The most efficient method of teaching facts is by reading, recitation, demonstration, drill, and testing. Although teaching the facts of science can sometimes be interesting, it *does not* reflect a true picture of the nature of science. The facts represent the product of science and minimize the importance of the processes that produced this product.

Students do not retain the facts for very long. (How many facts do you remember two weeks after a final exam?) Teaching only the facts of science gives the student the impression that science merely catalogues information. Moreover, when the process of how the facts were discoverd is ignored, the facts being taught cannot be fully understood. In essence, teaching the facts of science *does not* present children with the true picture or nature of science nor is it very exciting for children.

If teaching the facts gives a narrow view of science and results in poor retention, then perhaps teaching the concepts (major ideas) of science offers a better solution.

A concept is an idea that ties together many facts. A concept represents a link between many related facts. Here are some examples of science concepts:

All matter is made up of particles.
Living things are affected by their environment.
The celestial bodies move in predictable paths.
Matter changes state by absorbing or releasing energy.

Acquisition of concepts usually requires working with concrete objects, exploration, acquiring facts, and mentally manipulating ideas. It also requires more than memorization. The conceptual approach represents a truer picture of the nature of science than the factual approach mentioned earlier. Furthermore, the conceptual approach enables children to organize facts into a model or explanation about the nature of the universe.

Both factual and conceptual approaches to science teaching emphasize the *products* of science. These approaches *do not* include the processes or way in which these products were formulated.

The third way of teaching science is the process approach. A *process* approach to science teaching is based on the examination of what a *scientist does*. The processes are derived from an examination of what a scientist does and are called the *process skills of science*. Some of these process skills are: Observing, Measuring, Inferring, Manipulating Variables, Stating Hypotheses, Constructing Graphs and Tables of Data, Defining Operationally, and Carrying out Experiments.

In order to teach a child these process skills, it is necessary that he actually observe, measure, infer, manipulate variables, etc.; in short, that he act like a scientist. Or, in other words, that he does science. Therefore, this approach involves less reading about science and more involvement with concrete materials, i.e., more doing. The process approach gives children a valid understanding of the nature of science. The child can experience the excitement of science and can better understand its facts and concepts.

Teaching the process skills to children is having them *do* science, it is *not* telling. Whether you tell your students about science or allow books to do the telling you are doing just that: telling them about science. You are not giving them a chance to *feel* science. Teaching science by way of the process approach is "sciencing." And, most scientists and science educators feel that this is the best approach. Besides, children enjoy it because they are *active* and not passive learners.

What is unique about teaching science through the process approach is that it gives children a "feel" for science as well as enabling them to learn the facts and concepts of science. For example, it would be easy to tell children that water boils at 100°C or freezes at 0°C, but notice how more fruitful it would be to teach them how to measure temperature which is a science process skill. The children would be able to "discover" the boiling and freezing points of water on their own. They would get a "feel" for science. Note also that being able to measure temperature is transferable to many other related tasks. In other words, the child can measure the temperature of most anything now.

This is an important facet of the process approach to teaching science. The process skills you teach children are transferable to other tasks. Process skills are not isolated bits of knowledge like facts. They are broad skills that remain with children throughout life. A child may forget a concept or a fact like the boiling point of water but once he can measure temperature he will never forget how to perform this process skill.

Another example will clarify this idea of process skill transferability. Constructing graphs is a science process skill. A graph is a "picture" of the data a person has collected. It enables a person to interpret the data he has collected and thus to make inferences and conclusions. Once a child acquires the process skill of graphing he will be able to graph any kind of data both in science and in social studies or math. The skill is transferable to other science areas as well as to other disciplines.

In conclusion, science process skill development in children is a worthwhile endeavor. The science process skills are transferable to other areas and they are not easily forgotten. They give children a "feel" for the nature of science and enable children to "do" science. And, by "doing" science, children learn the facts and concepts of science. Thus, by using the process approach to teaching science, children learn the "processes" and "products" of science. Moreover, the process skill approach to teaching science is now emphasized in all recent elementary science textbook series and national science curricula.

There is one cautionary note. Before you as teachers can teach the science process skills to children you must possess these skills as well. That is the purpose of this book. This book is intended to develop your science process skills. Once you have these skills then teaching them to children will be an easier and more rewarding task.

The science process skills covered in this book are presented in two parts. The first part includes the basic science process skills which are intended for grades K-3. The basic skills are observing, inferring, measuring, communicating, classifying, and predicting. The integrated science process skills are intended for grades 4-6. The integrated skills are identifying variables, constructing tables of data, constructing graphs, describing relationships between variables, acquiring and processing data, analyzing investigations, constructing hypotheses, operationally defining variables, designing investigations, and experimenting.

PART 1

Basic Science Skills

The basic science skills represent nothing new in science in that they are the kinds of things all people do when they are sciencing. These skills are the springboard to science. The materials in this section were prepared with the following in mind: First, we as teachers both desire and are capable of doing a better job of teaching science, but first we must feel competent in science before attempting to develop science in our own students. Second, materials for doing good science need not be extraordinary. Good science can be learned with ordinary kinds of things. (In fact it is often the very ordinary that stimulates children to ask questions that lead them into fruitful inquiry.) Finally, newer science materials are responding to changes in methodology and philosophy. Almost all emphasize the development of science skills as a major goal. This requires getting children actively involved in learning science rather than learning about science.

The purpose of these materials is to help you develop some basic skills in science. Although the materials have been designed for the classroom teacher, many of the activities have been successfully used in elementary classrooms. The six basic skills developed by this program are: observing, classifying, predicting, measuring (metric of course), inferring, and communicating. Although the skills are interdependent, each section focuses on developing a specific skill area.

The materials have been designed for both independent and small group study. We do feel, however, that working through the materials with others enhances what you can learn. Each skill section includes: (1) a rationale and overview of the section, (2) specific objectives identifying the skills that you will be developing, (3) a series of practice activities to help develop the skills with self-checks so you can gauge your progress, (4) a mastery test so you can determine your level of mastery of the materials, and (5) practical suggestions and ideas for activities you can use to develop these same skills in students in your own classroom.

Procedures for Using the Materials

1. Read the objectives and purpose for each section.
2. Study the materials, do the practice activities, and check your answers with the self-checks provided.
3. Complete the mastery test at the end of the section and check your answers.
4. Continue working as you see fit. (While the ideas are still fresh in your mind you may want to try some of them out with your own class.)
5. Have fun sciencing!

B. C. by permission of Johnny Hart and Field Enterprises, Inc.

OBSERVATION 1

To do the Observation activities that follow you will need:

—a plant to observe
—a sugar cube
—a birthday candle
—a piece of clay
—matches
—a stick of chewing gum
—a meter stick or ruler
—an equal arm balance
—a set of masses

WHY IS OBSERVATION IMPORTANT?

    Through observation we learn about the fantastic world around us. We observe objects and natural phenomena through our five senses: sight, smell, touch, taste, and hearing.

    The information we gain leads to curiosity, questioning, thought, forming interpretations about our environment, and further investigation. Ability to observe is the most basic skill in science and is essential to the development of other science skills such as inferring, communicating, predicting, measuring, and classifying.

    The purpose of these exercises is to help you sharpen your skills of observation and learn what different kinds of observations you can make about your environment.

Performance Objectives:

After completing this set of activities you should:

1. given an object, substance, or event, be able to construct a list of qualitative and quantitative observations about that object, substance, or event. Your observations must be perceived through at least four of your senses.
2. given an event in which a change is involved, be able to construct a list of qualitative and quantitative observations about the change before, during, and after it occurs.

Activity 1

USING ALL YOUR SENSES

Observations are our perceptions of objects or natural events using our senses—sight, taste, smell, hearing and touch.

Go to one of the plants in the room and gather as much information as you can about the plant using all your senses. (CAUTION: Tasting any unknown substance is hazardous business; never taste anything unless you are absolutely certain that there is no danger involved.) Below, list at least ten observations about the plant. For each observation record the sense you used to obtain the information.

	Observation	**Sense**
1.		
2.		
3.		
4.		
5.		
6.		
7.		
8.		
9.		
10.		

Compare your observations with someone else's or check your observations with those that follow.

Self-check:

Your list of observations should provide at least enough information to answer these questions about the plant you observed:

1. What color is it? Is the color evenly distributed? (sight)?
2. Is the plant tall, short, spindly, sprawling? (sight)
3. Is there one main stem or many? (sight)
4. What is the general shape of the leaves? (sight)
5. Do the leaves have jagged or smooth edges? (sight, touch)
6. Are the leaves shiny or dull? (sight)
7. Are the leaves opposite one another or alternate? (sight)
8. Are the veins of the leaves distinct? Is there a central vein? Are the veins opposite one another or alternate? (sight)
9. Is the stem thick or thin? (sight, touch)
10. Are the leaves in clusters or separate? (sight)
11. What is the texture of the stem and leaf surfaces? (touch)
12. Do the leaves feel waxy? (touch)
13. Are the leaves stiff or easily pliable? (touch)
14. Does any part of the plant have an odor? (smell)
15. How does a leaf taste? (taste) If you are in any doubt about the safety in tasting, ask your instructor. Also, have mercy for the plant!

Activity 2

MAKING QUALITATIVE AND QUANTITATIVE OBSERVATIONS

Most of your observations in Activity 1 were probably qualitative observations; that is, you used only your senses to obtain the information. The following statements are examples of qualitative observations you might have made:

It is light green in color. (sight)
It has a pungent odor. (smell)
It tastes sour. (taste)
Its leaves are waxy and smooth. (touch)
It makes a rustling sound when lightly rubbed. (hearing)

Sometimes we want more precise information than our senses alone can give us and we include a reference to some standard unit of measure. When we refer to a standard unit of measure, we are making quantitative observations. Quantitative observations help us communicate specifics to others and provide a basis for comparisons. The following statements are examples of quantitative observations which could be made about some object:

It is 4 cm long and 2 cm wide. (metric ruler)
Its mass is 3 grams. (balance)
The temperature is 22°C. (thermometer)
This plant's leaves are clustered in groups of five.
This plant is larger than that plant.

Quantitative observations made with instruments such as rulers, meter sticks, balances, graduated cylinders or beakers, etc., give us specific and precise information. Although approximations and comparisons are not as precise, they are quantitative observations also.

Go to the observation supply area and pick up one of the small white cubes. In the chart that follows, list at least five qualitative observations and four quantitative observations about this object. For each qualitative observation identify which sense you used to gain the information and for each quantitative observation identify the instrument you used to aid your senses.

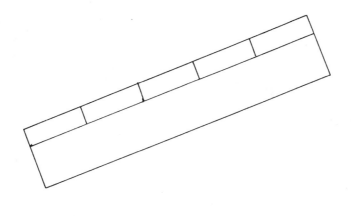

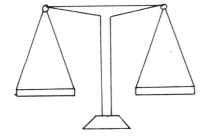

	Observations	Qualitative/Sense or Quantitative/Instrument
Qualitative	1. _____	_____
	2. _____	
	3. _____	
	4. _____	
	5. _____	
Quantitative	1. _____	
	2. _____	
	3. _____	
	4. _____	

Compare your answers with someone else's or check your answers with those that follow.

Self-check: Some of the observations you may have made are included in the following chart. Of course there are other acceptable observations. If you are in doubt about any of your observations, please ask.

Observations	Qualitative/Sense or Quantitative/Instrument
1. Object is cube shaped, white, sparkles.	Qual./Sight
2. Tastes sweet.	Qual./Taste
3. Has no distinctive odor.	Qual./Smell
4. Feels hard but crumbly; rough texture.	Qual./Touch
5. Makes a sharp sound when dropped.	Qual./Hearing
6. Length: 1.3 cm	Quant./Metric ruler
7. Width: 1.3 cm	Quant./Metric ruler
8. Height: 1.3 cm	Quant./Metric ruler
9. Mass: 2 grams	Quant./Balance

Activity 3

**OBSERVING
CHANGES**

You will often observe objects of phenomena that undergo physical or chemical changes. Your observations will be either qualitative, in which you use your senses to obtain information, or quantitative, in which you make a reference to some standard unit of measure. When asked to describe a change, it is important to include statements of observation made before, during, and after the change occurs.

Think, for example, about the changes you might observe to take place when you make popcorn. Before the kernel of corn is heated, it is teardrop shaped, about 1 cm × 1/2 cm × 1/2 cm in size, light brown in color, and has a hard, smooth shell. During the change (popping) the shell splits, a white puffy mass expands through the shell, and a short, light sound is produced. After the change the piece of popcorn is irregular in shape, about 3 cm × 2 cm × 3 cm in size, has a white, puffy texture, and a corn-like taste. Of course, more observations could be made.

Go to the observation supply area and pick up a birthday candle, a piece of clay for a base, and matches. In the chart below describe the candle before, during, and after it is burned. Include in your description at least seven (4 qualitative and 3 quantitative) observations before the change, three general statements about the changes as you observe them occurring, and five observations (4 qualitative and 1 quantitative) after the change has taken place. For each qualitative statement identify the sense you used to make the observation and for each quantitative observation identify the instrument you used to aid your senses.

	Qualitative Observations/Sense	**Quantitative Observations/Instrument**
Before	1. _____	1. _____
	2. _____	2. _____
	3. _____	3. _____
	4. _____	
During	1. _____	
	2. _____	
	3. _____	
After	1. _____	1. _____
	2. _____	
	3. _____	
	4. _____	

Compare your answers with someone else's or check your answers with the ones that follow. Then proceed to the mastery test.

Self-check: Below is a list of observations that could be made about a candle before it is lit, during burning, and after it has burned. Some of the observations will vary depending on the particular candle used. This, of course, is not a complete list. Please see your instructor if you have any questions about the observations you have made.

	Qualitative	Quantitative

Before

Qualitative
1. Color: white (sight)
2. Slight odor (smell)
3. Undetectable taste (taste)
4. Cylindrical shape (sight)
5. One end flat, other end cone shape (sight)
6. From cone extends a tuft of white, fuzzy, fibrous, soft material composed of strands (sight)
7. Each strand is cylindrical and irregularly coiled (sight)

Quantitative
1. Mass: 1-2 grams (bal.)
2. 5 cm long (metric ruler)
3. 5 mm diam. (metric ruler)
4. Each strand is .5 mm in diam. (metric ruler)
5. Coil of strands is 1 mm in diam. (metric ruler)
6. Coil extends 5 mm above tip of cone (metric ruler)

During

Qualitative
1. Fibrous strands turn black (sight)
2. Flame is elliptical in shape (sight)
3. Flame flickers in slight wind (sight)
4. Upper part of flame is bright yellow, lower part of flame is dull yellow with a blue margin (sight)
5. A puddle of liquid forms in place of the cone (sight)
6. Liquid material drips down side of candle; some solidifies on a cooler part of the candle, some drips to the table top (sight)

After

Qualitative
1. Color: white (sight)
2. Solid, irregular in shape (sight)
3. Small portion of fibrous strands protrude from mass
4. Exposed part of fibrous strands is black (sight)

Quantitative
1. Mass: 1/2-1 gram (bal.)
2. Height of mass at highest point—3 mm (metric ruler)
3. Distance across mass at widest point— 1 1/2 cm (metric ruler)

Observation Mastery Test

Go to the observation supply area and pick up a stick of chewing gum. In this test you will be observing chewing gum as it undergoes a change (chewing). In the chart below list at least nine statements of observation (5 qualitative and 4 quantitative) about the gum before you chew it, three qualitative statements about the changes you observe during chewing, and four statements of observation (3 qualitative and 1 quantitative) about the gum after it has been chewed for about two minutes. For each qualitative statement identify the sense you used to gain the information, and for each quantitative statement identify the instrument used to aid your senses. (For sanitary reasons please keep the gum on a piece of paper except when being chewed and dispose of the gum properly.)

	Qualitative Observations/Sense	**Quantitative Observations/Instrument**
Before	1. _____	1. _____
	2. _____	2. _____
	3. _____	3. _____
	4. _____	4. _____
	5. _____	
During	1. _____	
	2. _____	
	3. _____	
After	1. _____	1. _____
	2. _____	
	3. _____	

Compare your answers with someone else's or check your answers with those that follow.

Self-check: Below is a list of observations that could be made about chewing gum before, during, and after chewing. Of course this is not a complete list and some answers will vary with the particular type of gum used. Please see your instructor if you have any questions about the observations you have made.

	Qualitative	**Quantitative**
Before	1. Shape is rectangular (sight)	1. Length: 7 3/10 cm (metric ruler)
	2. Color: gray (sight)	2. Width: 2 cm (metric ruler)
	3. Cardboard-like texture (sight)	3. Thickness: 2 mm (metric ruler)
	4. Spearmint odor (smell)	4. Mass: 4 grams (balance/masses)
	5. Spearmint taste (taste)	
	6. Tears or breaks into smaller pieces when stretched (touch)	
	7. Easily bent with pressure of the fingers (touch)	

8. Has a pattern of short lines on broad surfaces (sight)
9. Has a fine powder-like substance on surfaces (sight, touch)

During

1. Becomes juicy and pliable in the mouth (touch)
2. Spearmint taste strong at first, then diminishes (taste)
3. Spearmint odor strong at first, then diminishes (smell)
4. Can be easily stretched apart with the tongue (touch)

After

1. Irregular shape, easily pliable (sight, touch)
2. Sticks to a dry surface (sight, touch)
3. Can be stretched into thin sheet-like strands (sight, touch)
4. Strands break and contract with further stretching (sight, touch)
5. Can be molded into different shapes with the fingers (sight, touch)

1. Mass: 1.5 grams (balance/masses)

Ideas for Your Classroom

1. Objects that can be interesting to observe are flowers, fruits, a pine cone, different kinds of leaves, feathers, and dried foods such as cereals.
2. Events such as popcorn popping, making ice cream, making butter or cookies can be delicious as well as informative.
3. A simple drop of water can be fascinating and lead to many challenging questions.
   Place a single drop of water on a paper towel or ordinary paper. What happens? (Water is attracted by paper fibers and is absorbed.)
   Place a drop of water on waxed paper. What happens? (The water drop "balls up"—cohesion.)
   Tip the waxed paper so that the drop moves. Does it roll or slide? How can you find out? (Hint: Sprinkle it with pepper or chalk dust.)
   Place a drop of water on plastic wrap. Place the plastic wrap so you can look at some printed material by peering through the water drop. What happens? (It magnifies.)
   Experiment with larger and smaller water drops to see which make better magnifiers.
4. Observation helps us learn that important changes are taking place.
   a. Seal one nail in a plastic sandwich bag and another nail in a plastic sandwich bag with a dampened paper towel. Observe for several days. What differences were observed? Why? An interesting spinoff of this lesson would be to come up with different ways to prevent the nail from rusting.
   b. A similar lesson could be conducted using bread. Students would learn that moisture is important for rotting to take place.
   c. Observing changes taking place with a banana peel in a sealed sandwich bag could lead to interest in how different kinds of foods are preserved. It could lead to an interesting history lesson. How did pioneers preserve food? What did those foods taste like?
5. "Our Senses Depending on Each Other" is an enjoyable lesson.
   Have the students close their eyes so they aren't peeking and plug their noses so they can't smell. Give them a small sliver of apple, then raw potato, then raw onion. Can the students taste the difference? Now let them do it with their noses unplugged. Now can they tell the difference? Why does the sense of smell help the sense of taste?

6. "Autumn and the Five Senses" would make an excellent theme for a bulletin board and interest center. Fruits and vegetables, the changing color of leaves, and other changes could be observed.

7. "Safety and Our Senses" is another topic that is worthy of teaching. One way to approach this topic is to use sense deprivation. For example, tape could be placed on the ends of the fingers and students could compare how sharp a tack feels between taped and untaped fingers. This lesson could be extended by imagining no sense of touch. How would we be protected from sharp objects, heat, sharp blows, or blisters on our feet? Smell warns us when we are breathing something that could be harmful to us. You could use vinegar to simulate noxious gases. Smelling smoke can also warn children of the danger of fire and being burned. The sense of taste can be discussed as something that can warn of danger, but stress the hazards of tasting unknown substances. This would be a good time to discuss with students some of the poisons and poisonous plants found in the home. Sight and hearing are more obvious as warners of danger (e.g. horns, traffic lights, etc.) but students still need to learn about safety. Again, the lesson could be started by having students imagine how they would cope with danger if they had no sense of sight or hearing. The school nurse or a local doctor could be invited to talk to students about eye and ear care and perform sight and hearing tests.

CLASSIFICATION 2

Most of the items you will need for classification are included in the activities themselves. Other activities will call for the following objects:

—two assortments of numbered buttons which are labeled:
  a) Multiple Properties
  b) Multi-Stage Classification
—an assortment of information panels from cereal boxes

WHY CLASSIFICATION IS IMPORTANT

For us to comprehend the overwhelming number of objects, events, and living things in the world around us, it is necessary to impose some kind of order. We impose order by observing similarities, differences, and interrelationships and grouping objects accordingly to suit some purpose. The basic requirement of any system of grouping is that it must be useful. Think of the number of classification schemes of which you are a member. Scientists classify you (man) for the purpose of study; the telephone company classifies you so that you can receive phone calls; your employer classifies you according to the work you do. Think of the ways the government classifies you (by sex, age, income, etc.). There are many classification systems you use almost daily: the "yellow pages," the classified section of the newspaper, the Dewey Decimal System in libraries, the systems for arranging items in grocery and department stores, and many more. As a teacher, you will be classifying students when you group them according to what they need to learn. Further, it is important to remember that classification is the process skill central to concept formation.

Goals: The purpose of these exercises is to help you learn to classify objects and events on the basis of observable characteristics.

Performance Objectives: After completing this set of activities, you should be able to:

1. given a set of objects, list observable properties which could be used to classify the objects and construct a binary classification system for each property.
2. given a set of objects, construct a multistage classification system and identify the properties on which the classification is based.
3. given a set of objects, identify properties by which the set of objects could be serially ordered and construct a serial order for each property.

Activity 1

**CONSTRUCTING
A BINARY
CLASSIFICATION
SYSTEM BASED
ON OBSERVABLE
PROPERTIES**

In a binary classification system the set of objects is divided into two subsets on the basis of whether each object has or does not have a particular property. To construct a binary classification system you must first identify a property which some of the objects have but all the others do not have. Then group all the objects displaying that property in one set and all the objects not displaying that property in another set. For example, biologists classify living things into two groups: animals and plants (plants being the group *not* displaying animal properties). Scientists further classify animals into two groups: those with backbones and those without backbones. When constructing a binary classification system be certain that all the objects in the original set will fit into one and only one of the two subsets. This is shown in the following activities.

Look at the set of "creatures" and observe their similarities and differences. In the left hand column of the chart provided, list at least three observable properties by which the creatures can be grouped into two subsets. In the "Yes" column write the numbers of the creatures that have the property that you have identified. In the "No" column, write the number or numbers of the creatures that lack the property that you have identified. Examine the following example.

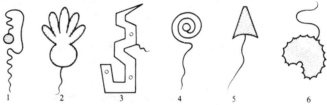

This drawing was reproduced from the Elementary Science Study Unit ATTRIBUTE GAMES AND PROBLEMS. Copyright © 1968 by Education Development Center, Inc.

Observable Properties	Yes	No
1. Speckled body (example)	1,5,6	2,3,4
2.		
3.		
4.		

Notice, as in the example, that for each property the subsets accommodate all the objects in the original set and that every object is assignable to one and only one of the subsets. Check to be certain your work in the preceding chart meets these two important requirements.

Compare your answers with someone else's or check your observations with those that follow.

Self-check:

Some of the properties you may have identified are as follows. Be certain that for each property the subsets accommodate all the objects in the original set and that every object is assignable to one and only one subset.

Observable Properties	Yes	No
1. (example) speckled body	1,5,6	2,3,4
2. round body	1,4	2,3,5,6
3. body with scalloped margin	6	1,2,3,4,5
4. striped body	2	1,3,4,5,6
5. body with circles	3	1,2,4,5,6
6. 3/4 of tail coiled	4	1,2,3,5,6

Activity 2

USING MULTIPLE PROPERTIES

Binary classification also can be used when you wish to group objects together that have more than one property in common.

Go to the supply area and pick up the sets of buttons labeled "Multiple Properties". What are some ways the buttons can be grouped using multiple characteristics?

1. _____

2. _____

3. _____

Self-check:

Answers will vary. They could include:

1. Red buttons with two holes.
2. White buttons with four holes.
3. Blue buttons with rough edges.
4. The answers could be more subtle. For example, one set could be red and blue buttons with two holes and smooth edges.

A good way to sharpen this binary classification skill is through the "Button Game." Get a partner. The rules for this game are quite simple.

1. Make up a rule for grouping the buttons into two sets.
2. Group the buttons according to your rule.
3. See if your partner can guess the rule.
4. When your partner guesses this rule, he or she gets to make up the rule, group the buttons, and then let you guess.

Activity 3

**CONSTRUCTING
A MULTI-STAGE
CLASSIFICATION
SYSTEM**

In a multi-stage classification system the set of objects is sorted again and again so that a hierarchy of sets and subsets is established. As in a binary scheme, subsets are determined by sorting objects that have a particular property from those that do not have that property. Animals, for example, are classified as either having backbones or not having backbones. Those having backbones can be further classified as either having hair or not having hair.

Because you are already familiar with the "creatures" in Activity 1, we will use them to illustrate how a multi-stage classification system is constructed. Notice that the scheme identifies the observable properties by which the items are sorted and that each item associated with the properties is identified.

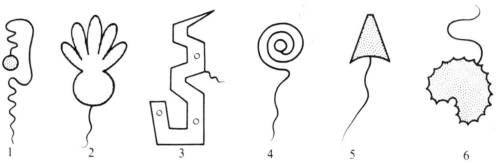

1   2   3   4   5   6

This drawing was reproduced from the Elementary Science Study Unit ATTRIBUTE GAMES AND PROBLEMS. Copyright   1968 by Education Development Center, Inc.

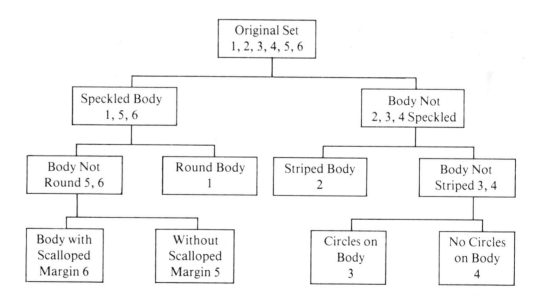

In addition to the characteristics already discussed, a multi-stage classification system has the following features:

1. Several other schemes may be possible depending upon which observable properties are used for grouping.
2. When each object in the original set is separated into a category by itself the scheme is complete.
3. A unique description of each object can be obtained by listing all the properties that the object has. In the above scheme, for example, creature 6 can be distinguished from the other creatures in the original set by listing its properties; body is speckled, not round, but has a scalloped margin.

Now it's your turn. Use the numbered button assortment called "Multi-Stage Classification" to complete the system started below. In each box, indicate the property such as color, number of holes, size, etc. that you used to make the grouping. Be sure to carry the scheme through to completion. When the scheme is completed, each button will be in a box by itself.

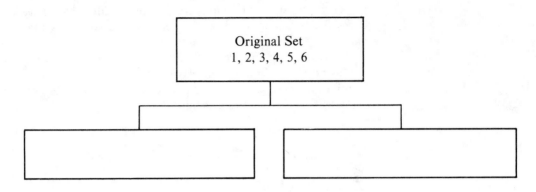

Self-check: There are many possible schemes depending on the buttons' characteristics and the order in which you selected them. If in doubt, ask your instructor.

For additional practice, construct a multi-stage classification system for the following set of creatures on a separate sheet of paper. Identify the property you use for each grouping by labeling the boxes and listing the numbers of creatures displaying that property. Again, be sure to carry the scheme through to completion; that is, each member of the original set must be in a category by itself.

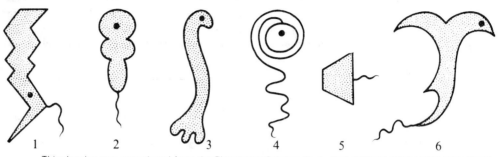

This drawing was reproduced from the Elementary Science Study Unit ATTRIBUTE GAMES AND PROB-LEMS. Copyright © by Education Development Center, Inc.

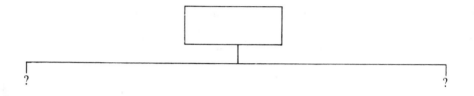

Self-check: Compare your scheme with someone else's or the one following. Remember, other schemes are possible. Your scheme depends on the properties you select and the order in which you select them.

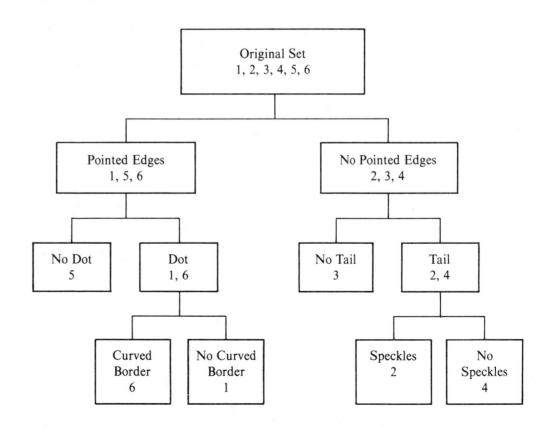

Activity 4

SERIAL ORDERING   It sometimes is necessary to order objects according to the extent to which they display a particular property. Depending upon the purpose of the classification, objects may be ordered on the basis of size, shape, color, or a variety of other characteristics. In a hardware store, nails are ordered on the basis of size. Paints can be arranged according to size of can, color, and hue. Clothing stores use size to arrange merchandise in serial order.

Go to the supply area and obtain the information panels from cereal boxes. Examine them and identify three properties by which these panels could be arranged in order.

1. _____

2. _____

3. _____

Self-check: Answers will vary. They could include:

1. Number of calories per serving
2. Amount of iron per serving
3. Amount of thiamin per serving
4. Amount of protein per serving

Serial order the panels according to three properties in the chart below. Place the name of the property in the left column and serial order the panels in the right column. (You may want to number the information panels for convenience.)

Property	**Serial Order**
_____	_____
_____	_____
_____	_____

Self-check: Compare your answers with someone else's.

Classification Mastery Test

For this test you will construct (a) a binary classification system, (b) a multi-stage classification system, and (c) a serial order classification system for the following set of "creatures":

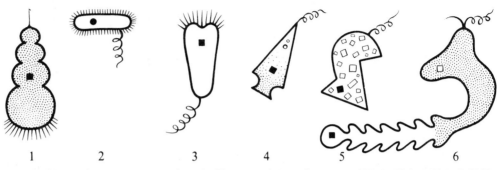

This drawing was reproduced from the Elementary Science Study Unit ATTRIBUTE GAMES AND PROBLEMS. Copyright © 1968 by Education Development Center, Inc.

a. In the chart below identify at least three observable properties by which these creatures could be classified in a binary classification system. In the proper column indicate which creatures have or do not have each property.

Observable Property	Yes	No
1.		
2.		
3.		

b. Construct at least one multi-stage classification system for these "creatures" and carry it through to completion. In each box identify the property used for grouping and list the number of each "creature" with that property.

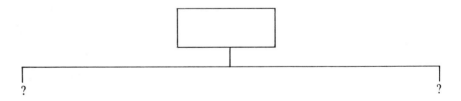

Check your answers to parts (a) and (b) with those that follow. Be sure to do part (c) in the Self-check.

Self-check: a. Some observable properties on which binary classification systems for these "creatures" could be based are listed below:

Observable Property	Yes	No
1. Speckled Body	1,4,6	2,3,5
2. Hair-like projections on body	1,2,3	4,5,6
3. Curly "tail"	2,3,4,5,6	1
4. Black square on body	1,3,4,5,6	2
5. Body margin with at least one straight line	4,5	1,2,3,6

b. One possible multi-stage classification system for this set of "creatures" is shown below. Several other schemes are possible depending on which properties are used for grouping. If you have questions about your classification scheme compare it with someone else's or see your instructor.

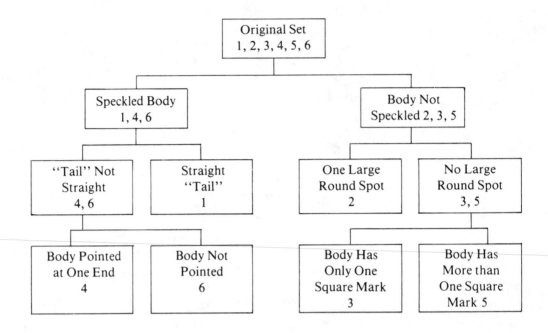

c. In the chart below identify at least two properties by which these "creatures" could be serially ordered. Then serial order the "creatures" on the basis of each property by listing the numbers in the proper order.

Observable Property	Serial Order
1.	
2.	

Compare your answers with someone else's or check your answers with those that follow.

Self-check: d. Some possible ways of serial ordering these "creatures" are listed below. Other ways may be possible depending upon which properties are used as a basis for the classification.

Observable Property	Serial Order
1. Size of body	smallest—largest 2,4,3,5,1,6
2. Number of spots	least—most 2,3,5,4,1,6
3. Number of projections extending from body	least—most 4,5,6,3,1,2

Ideas for Your Classroom

1. Water play is an enjoyable activity for the young learners. In one set of activities, students can compare objects that sink with objects that float. (This is a building block for later concepts of density and buoyancy.)

   In another set of activities, students can predict the serial order of the volumes of empty containers and check their prediction by filling the containers, one with the others. (In doing this, they learn how to relate sizes and shapes with volumes of containers.)

2. Liquids vary in density and this affects their buoyant properties. A neat puzzle for older children is to present them with two containers of water: one in which a hard boiled egg is floating and the other in which the hard boiled egg is resting on the bottom. (The only difference between the glasses of water is that one contains a few tablespoons of dissolved salt.)

3. Animals are grouped on the basis of similarities and differences. Ways in which they may be grouped include: how they obtain their food; whether thay lay eggs or bear live young; by their habitat (parks, forests, oceans, ponds, and so on) or how they protect themselves. Have you ever wondered why a zebra had stripes?

   Collect pictures of various animals and explore the various ways they can be classified using binary classifications. If your class feels really ambitious, they may construct a multi-stage classification system for animals. (You may want to limit their efforts to local kinds of animals because the entire animal kingdom is a gigantic multi-stage classification system.)

4. Plants can be used for binary and multi-stage classification as well as serial ordering. Plant leaves are excellent for binary and multi-stage classification. Trees, for example, could be serial ordered by the distance around, height, age (by counting the rings) and a number of other ways.

   One interesting project would be to investigate how plants disperse their seeds: some rely on the wind; some need animals to eat their fruit; some "hitch" rides on animals; just to mention a few. Further, examine the similarities and differences of plant seeds dispersed in the same manner. Maple seeds and dandelions are both spread by the wind but their methods are different. Dandelion seeds could be likened to parachutes and maple seeds could be compared to helicopters.

5. Is it natural or man-made? Some fabrics from which clothes are made occur naturally while others are manufactured from other products like petroleum.

6. Nutrition is a natural unit to practice classification skills. Besides studying the food groups, you can have your students read the sugar content of various cereals and measure out equivalent amounts of sugar. (Sand or salt may be substituted to give the same visual effect at a lower cost.) Once the amounts have been measured out, they can be ordered.

B. C. by permission of Johnny
Hart and Field Enterprises, Inc.

COMMUNICATION 3

For the Communication activities that follow you will need a set of tangrams. A tangram is a Chinese puzzle made by cutting a square into five triangles, a square, and a rhomboid. The pieces are used to form different figures and designs. You will use the set of tangrams on page 199 for Activity 1.

WHY COMMUNICATION IS IMPORTANT

Our ability to communicate with others is basic to everything we do. Graphs, charts, maps, symbols, diagrams, mathematical equations, and visual demonstrations, as well as the written or spoken word, are all methods of communication used frequently in science. Effective communication is clear, precise, and unambiguous and uses skills which need to be developed and practiced. As teachers we attempt to influence behavior through the written or spoken word. We all have a need to express our ideas, feelings, and needs to others, and we begin to learn early in life that communication is basic to problem solving.

Goals:

These exercises will help you learn to communicate ideas, directions, and descriptions effectively and give you practice in using and constructing various methods of communication.

Performance Objectives:

After completing this set of materials, you should be able to:

1. describe an object or event in sufficient detail so that another person can identify it.
2. construct a map showing relative distances, positions, and sizes of objects with sufficient accuracy so that another person can locate a particular place or object using the map.

**Describing Objects
to Another Person:**

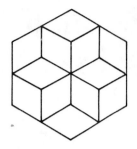

Look at the figure above. Suppose you were asked to describe this figure to someone in sufficient detail so that he could draw it from your description. The drawer would need to know what kind of lines to draw, where to place them, and how long they should be. How would *you* describe it? Look at the figure again and keep looking at it until you perceive it in a different way than you did at first glance. (There are at least eight different ways to perceive this figure.) The way you describe something to someone else depends on how *you* perceive it.

When you describe an object or event to someone your purpose will be better served if your communication is an effective one. You can communicate effectively if you:

1. describe only what you observe (see, feel, smell, hear, and taste) rather than what you infer about the object or event.
2. make your description brief by using precise language.
3. communicate information accurately using as many qualitative observations as the situation may call for.
4. consider the point of view and past experience of the person with whom you are communicating.
5. provide a means for getting "feedback" from the person with whom you are communicating in order to determine the effectiveness of your communication.
6. construct an alternative description if necessary.

Activity 1

GIVING AND FOLLOWING DIRECTIONS

B. C. by permission of Johnny
Hart and Field Enterprises, Inc.

Go to the communication supply area and pick up a set of tangrams or cut them out of page 199. Select a partner and be sure that both of you have identical sets of tangrams. Sit with your partner and erect a screen or barrier so you cannot see each other's tangrams. Make a design with your tangrams. (It is not necessary to use all the pieces.) Giving precise directions to your partner, tell him where to place each of his tangrams so that his design looks exactly like yours. How effectively you communicate with your partner will be measured by the closeness of similarity between the designs when your directions are completed. Do this activity a second time and see if your skills of communication improve.

You may wish to identify the specific areas of giving directions which gave you some trouble so that you can practice and improve in these areas. Use the space below to make notes for yourself.

—Describing only what is observed:

—Making descriptions brief:

—Using precise language:

—Communicating information accurately:

—Considering another's point of view or position:

Activity 2

**COMMUNICATING
DESCRIPTIONS**

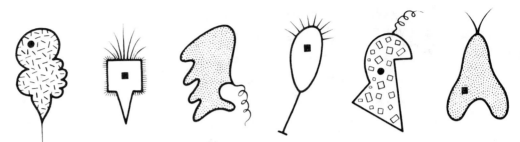

This drawing was reproduced from the Elementary Science Study Unit ATTRIBUTE GAMES AND PROB-
LEMS. Copyright © 1968 by Education Development Center, Inc.

Look at the set of "creatures" above. Select one of the creatures to describe to your
partner but do not tell which one you have selected. Compose an accurate and complete
description of the creature so that your partner can recognize the creature you are describing. Your partner should be able to recognize the creature quickly and easily from your
description.

Here is another set of creatures:

This drawing was reproduced from the Elementary Science Study Unit ATTRIBUTE GAMES AND PROB-
LEMS. Copyright © 1968 by Education Development Center, Inc.

Select one of these creatures to describe but do not tell your partner which one you
have chosen. Your partner should have paper and pencil ready. This time the "feedback" of
your communication will be a drawing which your partner will make from your description
and directions. Communicate to your partner precisely what you observe about the creature
and give careful directions to guide your partner smoothly through the drawing. If your
communication is an effective one the drawing will look very similar to the original and your
partner will have made the drawing without hesitation or confusion about your directions.

Activity 3

**COMMUNICATING
WITH MAPS**

Some directions can be effectively communicated only with the use of maps. (Actually mathematical formulas, patterns, guides, floorplans, blueprints, photographs, schematic drawings, and descriptions are all maps.) A map is any symbolic representation. To be useful a map must have:

1. a title, telling what the map is about.
2. symbols, representing places or objects.
3. a key, telling what each symbol represents.
4. a scale, showing relative distances and sizes of objects.

Suzanne wanted to tell her classmates about her trip to one of the islands of Hawaii. She drew a map of the island and labeled all the places on the map that she visited. Then she used the map to show the class where she had been and what she did there. By placing numbers along the top of the map and letters along the side of the map, she found it was easier to tell her classmates where places were located. Diamond Head (a once active volcano), for example, is located at about H—7. That is the place on the map close to where lines drawn from H and 7 would cross. Now it is your turn.

Below Suzanne's map is a list of fun things she did and places she went on Oahu. For each place listed, locate its position on the map and identify its location by naming the appropriate letter and number on the map.

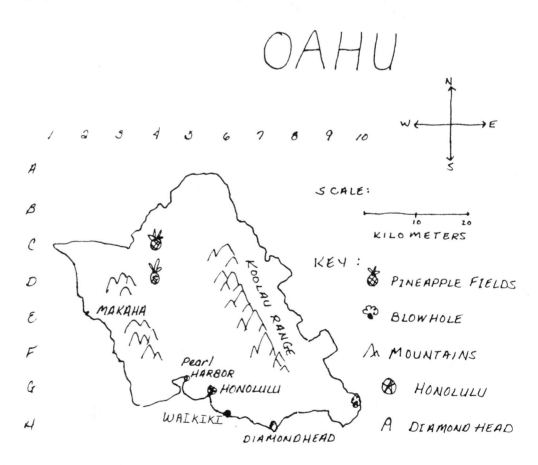

1. _____ visited the pineapple fields

2. _____ saw the monument at Pearl Harbor

3. _____ saw the geyser of water erupting from the Blow Hole

4. _____ went surfing at the beach of Makaha

5. _____ went swimming and snorkeling at Waikiki Beach

Self-check: 1. C—4 and D—4
2. G—5
3. H—10
4. E—2
5. H—6

Communication Mastery Test

A. Place three objects somewhere in the room and write a description of one of the objects.
B. Construct a map of the room so that a person can find each of the objects.
C. Give your map and description to someone in your class and have them locate and recognize the object desired. If the person using your map and description finds and recognizes the object in just one attempt then you know your communication is an effective one. Give yourself a pat on the back!

Ideas for Your Classroom

1. Although it was not covered in this chapter, writing is a very important communication skill. Good clear writing like clear verbal communication must be practiced. One way this can be practiced in science is to have students write what they are learning, especially during activities. You may want to adopt a format similar to the one below:

   a. We were studying _____

   b. We did _____

   c. We observed _____

   d. We learned _____

2. A game that will help students' descriptive skills is similar to one earlier in the chapter. Place two or three students in each group. Let one student pick out an object in the room and describe it to the others. (The description should be observations rather than function; that is, it is red rather than you write with it.) When the object is correctly identified, then another student gets a turn.

3. An interesting application of communication skills to social studies would be to obtain an old map of your geographic area and a current map. If you are lucky enough to get a map of your area when your state adopted its seal (excepting Hawaii and Alaska), you get a bonus. Compare the maps. What changes have taken place? What used to be where you are now? Where is your home? Now for the bonus . . . Your state seal is a piece of communication. When it was adopted, the people of the state were trying to communicate the state's important qualities at that time. Have these qualities changed? If you were going to design a state seal, what would you include now?

4. *Using our Resources*

   a. "Where does it originate?" is an interesting question for a study. Bulletin boards and activities could be used to help students gain an appreciation and understanding of how we use our environment to meet our needs. Many children need to learn that stores are not the sources of eggs, milk, pencils, baseball bats, and clothes. In a study of the sources of foods, chains could be constructed to show events between the producers and consumers. (The chains could vary in level to fit the sophistication of the students.) If desired, steps could be added to illustrate processing, transportation, sales or any other event between the raw product and the consumer.

   Where does electricity originate? When you turn on a switch, does the electricity come from a local plant or one far away? What kind of plant generates the electricity? What kinds of energy transformations take place between its production and use? As you use electricity, what kinds of energy transformations take place?

   b. "Where does it go?" is another question worth studying. What happens to things we "throw away"? This could lead to a study of waste disposal and some of its problems as well as a study of recycling. While "What happens when I flush the toilet?" may not be one of the burning questions in your life, it might be worth exploring.

5. "Gossip" is an interesting game that helps improve communication skills. You could start the game by having the students form a circle. Then you give a short written message to one of the students. The student reads the message and whispers it once to his or her neighbor, who in turn passes the message along verbally. When the message has gone around the circle, the last student says the message aloud. Compare the original message with it. This could lead to a discussion of how we receive information. Perhaps it would be possible to visit a radio or television station or newspaper office. If that's not possible, maybe they have a speaker that could visit your class.

6. "Kidnap" is another game that can improve observation and communication skills. Have three students, one victim and two villains, perform the following skit. Dressed in special clothes, the masked villains kidnap the victim (also dressed in unique garb) quickly from the room. Have the class write a brief eyewitness account, describing the event and the descriptions of the victim and kidnappers. Compare the results. You might have a person from the police visit the class to talk about accuracy of communication and being an eyewitness.

7. Labels communicate! Have your students become label readers. Find out the contents of junk foods or any other food that comes in a container. What other products have labels? What does the label tell about the product?

8. Advertisements are another form of communication. Have your students study different advertisements from different sources: television, magazines, newspapers, etc. What are they communicating? Are there hidden messages?

METRIC MEASUREMENT 4

To do the Metric Measurement activities that follow you will need:

—a meter stick
—a metric ruler
—an equal-arm balance
—a set of masses
—20 centicubes
—a baby food jar (about 140 ml)
—3 large sinkers (about 28 g each)
—a liter container
—4 containers in various sizes and shapes
—a graduated cylinder
—5 marbles
—4 washers (about this size:
—ice cubes
—a Celsius thermometer

For the Mastery Test you will need a "Measurement Test Packet" containing:

—a toothpick
—a string of washers

WHY METRIC MEASUREMENT IS IMPORTANT

How much? How far? What size? How long? How many? How fast? These are questions with which we deal every day and we need to be able to handle them with ease. Well developed skills in measuring are essential in making quantitative observations, classifying and comparing things around us, and communicating effectively to others. The change to the metric system of measurement should not be viewed as a problem but rather as a solution to many problems. The metric system gives us easy to learn units for everyday use, and multiplying and dividing are relatively easy operations since the metric system is in base ten. Our conversion to the metric system will also give us uniformity with other countries with which we trade and communicate.

Goals: In these exercises you will learn and practice skills needed to do measurements in the metric system. As you develop these skills you should begin to think metric.

Performance Objectives: After completing this set of activities, you should be able to:

1. select the appropriate metric unit for measuring any property (length, volume, temperature, mass, and weight) of a given object.
2. given a set of metric units, state equivalent metric measures using prefixes (perform conversions in the metric system).
3. measure the temperature, length, volume, mass, or force of any object to the nearest .1 unit.

Activity 1

**BASIC UNITS
OF MEASURE**

The three most frequently used measures in the metric system are the *meter, liter,* and *kilogram.* Meters are used to measure lengths or distances, liters are used to measure volumes, and kilograms are used to measure mass.

Write under each object shown below whether it should be measured in meters, liters, or kilograms.

Reprinted from the METRIC SYSTEM: BOOK 3 by Diane Rabenau. Copyright © 1974 by Milliken Publishing Company. Used by permission of the publisher.

Compare your answers with those in the Self-check.

Self-check:

gasoline: liters
tree: meters
milk: liters
apples: kilograms
potatoes: kilograms
butter: kilograms
fence: meters
apple cider: liters
grape juice: liters
football field: meters
sugar: kilograms
baseball field: meters

Activity 2

METRIC PREFIXES   One day you'll be saying "Give them a centimeter and they'll take a kilometer." and "A gram of prevention is worth a kilogram of cure." As strange as the language may seem now, one of the advantages of the metric system is its terminology. Instead of remembering conversions like 12 inches equals one foot equals one-third yards equals 1/5280 mile, the metric system uses *prefixes* to indicate larger and smaller quantities. By adding prefixes to the basic units of measure (meter, liter, and gram), you can indicate larger and smaller quantities.

The most frequently used prefixes are:

Prefix	**Prefix Meaning**
kilo	1000 times the base unit
hecto	100 times the base unit
deka (deca)	10 times the base unit
deci	1/10 of the base unit
centi	1/100 of the base unit
milli	1/1000 of the base unit

The metric system is much like our monetary system in that both are decimal (based on ten) systems. For example:

$$\text{just as . . . 1 dollar} = \text{10 dimes, or 100 cents,}$$
$$\text{so . . . 1 meter} = \text{10 decimeters, or}$$
$$\text{100 centimeters}$$

You will be using the prefixes with each of the metric base units so spend a few minutes right now getting to know them and their meanings. Then do the practice exercise that follows.

Use your knowledge of the prefixes and their meanings to answer the following questions:

1. A decade is a period of _____ years.

2. A decapod is an animal which has _____ legs.

3. In the decimal system, .5 is read as five _____ .

4. A hectometer equals _____ meters.

5. A kilowatt equals _____ watts.

6. If a centipede has as many legs as its name implies, each leg is _____ (what part) of the total number of legs.

7. On the centigrade (Celsius) temperature scale each degree is _____ (what part) of the scale.

8. In a millennium, each year is _____ (what part) of the total period of time.

9. A mill is _____ (what part) of a dollar.

Check your answers with the ones in the Self-check.

Self-check: 1. decade: 10 (deka or deca) years
2. decapod: 10 (deka or deca) legs
3. decimal: tenths (deci meaning tenth)
4. hectometer: 100 (hecto) meters
5. kilowatt: 1000 (kilo) watts
6. centipede: 1/100 (centi)
7. centigrade: 1/100 (centi)
8. millennium: 1/1000 (milli)
9. mill: 1/1000 (milli) of a dollar

Activity 3

**MEASURING
METRIC LENGTHS**

The *meter* is the basic unit for measuring length in the metric system. A meter is about the distance from your nose to the tip of your longest finger—

Head is turned in the opposite direction.

The symbol "m" is used to stand for meter.

Go to the supply area and pick up a meter stick. Carefully observe the length of the meter stick, then close your eyes and try to picture that length in your mind. Look around the room and try to select some things which you think are about one meter in length. Then use the meter stick to check your predictions. When you are through you should have a good picture in mind of how long a meter really is.

Predict the following lengths to the nearest meter and record them in the column labeled "Predict." Then *measure* each of the lengths to the nearest meter and record the measurements in the "Measure" column.

	Predict	**Measure**
Length of instructor's table		
Width of the instructor's table		
Width of the doorway		
Height of the doorway		
Distance from floor to window sill		

If your predictions and measurements are fairly close, you are beginning to think metric!!

Compare your measurements with someone else's.

You may already have noticed that it may be difficult to measure distances much longer or shorter than one meter using a meter stick. Distances longer or shorter than one meter can be described by using the meter prefixes.

Distances much shorter than a meter can be measured using a metric ruler.

Now examine the meter stick and find the millimeter, centimeter and decimeter marks on it.

The *millimeter* marks are about as wide as the wire in a paper clip. It is about the distance between two legs of the letter "m." It takes 10 millimeters to make a centimeter. Millimeter is symbolized mm.

The *centimeter* marks are about the same length as the width of a paper clip or the width of your little finger. It takes 100 centimeters to make a meter. Centimeter is symbolized cm.

The *decimeter* is a little longer than the width of your hand or about the length of a new piece of chalk. It takes 10 decimeters to make a meter.

Use the following scales to compare these lengths. Again, try to picture in your mind how long millimeters, centimeters, and decimeters really are.

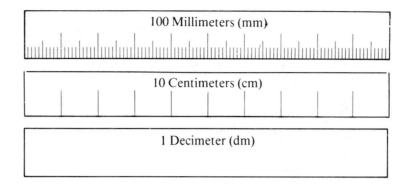

Now let's see if you can put what you have learned to use.
Suppose you are asked to measure this line:

You should carefully lay your metric ruler along the line like this:

|||||||||||||||||||||||||||||||||||||||||||||||||||||||||||||||||||||||||||||||||||||||||||||||||
0   1   2   3   4   5   6   7   8   9   10   11   12   13

Notice that the line measures more than 5 but less than 6 centimeters. If you were to measure this line to the nearest centimeter, you would say it is 6 cm long since it is closer to 6 cm than to 5 cm. More precisely the line measures seven millimeter marks beyond 5 cm. Rather than saying 5 cm, 7 mm you should say 5.7 centimeters, or 57 mm. It is considered bad form to mix metric units. When measuring you will have to decide, or be told, how precisely you should measure.

For practice . . .

On the scale below, identify and label 1 mm, 1 cm, and 1 dm. Then complete the following metric statements.

|||||||||||||||||||||||||||||||||||||||||||||||||||||||||||||||||||||||||||||||||||||||||||||||||
0   1   2   3   4   5   6   7   8   9   10   11   12   13

1. 1 meter = ____ decimeters = ____ centimeters = ____ millimeters.

2. 1 dm = ____ cm = ____ mm.

3. 1 mm = ____ m = ____ dm = ____ cm.

4. This page measures ____ centimeters wide. (Measure to the nearest cm.)

5. To the nearest .1 of a centimeter, this page is ____ cm long.

Check your answers with the ones following

Self-check: 1. 1 mm = 10 dm = 100 cm = 1000 mm
2. 1 dm = 10 cm = 100 mm
3. 1 mm = 1/1000 m = 1/100 dm = 1/10 cm or = .001 m = .01 dm = .1 cm
4. 22 cm
5. 27.9 cm

What about measuring longer distances?

Distances longer than a few meters can be measured using a metric tape or wheel calibrated in meters, centimeters, and millimeters. Students have more fun, and learn more, using measuring devices they have made themselves.

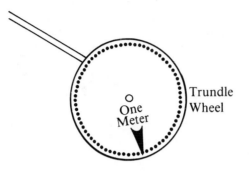

Distances of several meters may be measured in dekameters or hectometers, although these units are not frequently used.

The *dekameter* is a measure of length equal to 10 meters. Its symbol is dam.

The *hectometer* is a measure of length equal to 100 meters. Its symbol is hm.

A race covering a distance of 500 meters is more likely to be called a 500 meter race than a 50 dekameter race or a 5 hectometer race.

For long distances . . .

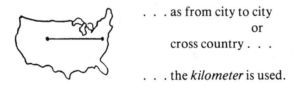

. . . as from city to city

or

cross country . . .

. . . the *kilometer* is used.

The kilometer is a measure of length equal to 1000 meters. Its symbol is km. It would take about 15 minutes to walk a kilometer. The length of nine football fields placed end to end would be about one kilometer. Kilometers can be measured using the distance measuring gauge, called an odometer, in a car. Maps drawn to metric scale can help you determine long distances.

For practice . . .

1. 2 km = _____ m

2. 3 km = _____ m

3. 4000 m = _____ km

4. 21,000 m = _____ km

5. 2 dam = _____ m

6. 500 m = _____ hm

7. 1 km = _____ dam

8. 1 km = _____ hm

Fill in the missing information in the following chart. The middle column asks you to identify the instrument(s) used to measure each distance and the right column asks you to name the units in which each distance is measured.

If you want to measure . . .	You should use a . . .	And measure in . . .
long distances (as from place to place or city to city)		
average distances (as short as one step or as long as several football fields)		
short distances (as short as the width of a finger or as long as a step)		
very small distances (less than the width of a finger) or *very precise measurements* (accurate to a very small unit)		

Compare your answers for the practice exercise with those on the following chart.

Self-check:

1. 2 km = 2000 m
2. 3 km = 3000 m
3. 4000 m = 4 km
4. 21,000 m = 21 km

5. 2 dam = 20 m
6. 500 m = 5 hm
7. 1 km = 100 dam
8. 1 km = 10 hm

If you want to measure . . .	You should use a . . .	And measure in . . .
long distances (as from place to place or city to city)	metric odometer (a gauge on a car) or a map (with a metric scale)	kilometers (km)
average distances (as short as one step or as long as several football fields)	meter stick, metric tape, or metric measuring wheel	meters (m)
short distances (as short as the width of a finger or as long as a step)	metric ruler	centimeters (cm)
very small distances (less than the width of a finger) or *very precise measurements*	metric ruler	millimeters (mm)

Activity 4

**MEASURING
METRIC MASSES**

First a word about *mass* and *weight* . . .

There is a very definite difference between mass and weight—while weight refers to how heavy an object is, mass refers to how much stuff, or matter, the object is made of. The problem lies in the fact that people often talk about weight when they really mean mass. Consequently, in the everyday implementation of the metric system, mass and weight are being treated as if they were the same; that is, they both use the gram as their base unit. Where it is not necessary for you to make the distinction between mass and weight, the following discussion about mass may also apply to weight. For a more scientific approach to measuring metric weights, see *Measuring Forces*.

The metric base unit of mass (weight) is the gram. How much is a gram?

 . . . the mass of the water this cube can hold is 1 gram.

 Hold a nickel in your hand and try to get a "feel" of its mass. Its mass is about 5 grams.

Masses larger or smaller than the gram can be described using the prefixes with the basic unit. The *kilogram* is the unit most used in measuring large masses. One kilogram is equal to 1000 grams and is the mass of one liter of water. An average man might mass about 80 kg. Very large masses are measured in *metric tons*. One metric ton is the mass of 1000 kilograms.

Masses smaller than the gram are measured in *milligrams*. To get an idea of how small one milligram is, pick up a postage stamp and think about the fact that it masses about 20 milligrams.

To find the mass of objects, we use the equal-arm balance, like the one pictured below. We do so by placing the object of unknown mass on one side and balancing it with objects of known mass on the other side.

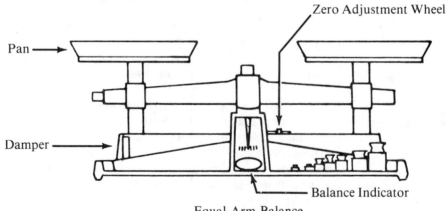

Zero Adjustment Wheel

Pan →

Damper →

Balance Indicator

Equal-Arm Balance

Before massing an object, always be sure the balance you are using is "zeroed." This means that the two empty pans are in balance. If the balance is zeroed, the balance indicator will point to the exact center of its scale. If the indicator is off center, turn the *zero adjustment wheel* slightly until the indicator does point to the center of its scale. This zero adjustment wheel simply corrects for an out of balance condition. If the balance is not zeroed prior to massing, your results will not be accurate.

On the left side of the base is a small projection which on some balances resembles a paper clip. This is the *damper*. By pushing the damper toward the center of the balance you can lessen any up and down movement of the pans due to vibration of air currents in the room.

Stored at the base of the balance are the *standard gram masses*. These masses are the objects of known mass with which objects of unknown mass are compared. Simply place the object of unknown mass in one pan, then add masses to the other pan until the pans balance and the indicator registers center. The mass of the unknown is the total of the masses it took to balance the pans.

And now a checklist for the procedure and some practice massing with an equal-arm balance.

To mass an object, follow this procedure:

1. *Zero* the equal-arm balance; use the damper if necessary.
2. If you are massing out chemicals, *cover* the pan with a small piece of paper so that the balance is kept clean.
3. *Place the object* you wish to mass on one of the pans.
4. *Add masses* to the other pan until the balance arms are horizontal.
5. *Total the masses* it took to balance the unknown mass.
6. *Record* the observed mass.

Obtain from the supply area an equal-arm (double-pan) balance, 20 centicubes, a baby food jar, three large sinkers, and a set of masses. Find the mass of the objects as described in the chart below and record your findings in the column labeled "Your Masses." In order that you may have a check for your measurements we have massed the same objects and recorded "our masses" in the chart. Slight differences may occur so you will have to exercise some judgment in comparing your masses with ours.

Object	Our Masses	Your Masses
5 centicubes	5 grams	
20 centicubes	20 grams	
baby food jars	84 grams	
three sinkers	85 grams	

Select three relatively small items in the lab. Pick each one up and try to guess its mass. Then check your prediction using the equal-arm balance. Record the name of the object, your guess, and the actual mass in the table below.

Object	Predicted Mass	Observed Mass
1.		
2.		
3.		

Are you thinking metric?!

Pull your thoughts about measuring metric masses together and fill in the following chart:

If you want to measure . . .	You should use a . . .	And measure in . . .
mass of relatively large objects (about the size of a Hi C can or package of Velveeta cheese and larger)		
mass of relatively small objects (between the size of a coin and the size of a coffee can)		
very small masses (such as vitamins and pills)		

Compare your chart with the following one.

Self-check:

If you want to measure . . .	You should use . . .	And measure in . . .
mass of relatively large objects (about the size of a Hi C can or package of Velveeta cheese and larger)	a scale or compare with known masses	kilograms (kg)
mass of relatively small objects (between the size of a coin and the size of a coffee can)	an equal-arm balance	grams (g)
very small masses (such as vitamins and pills)	an equal-arm balance which is very sensitive	milligrams (mg)

Activity 5

MEASURING METRIC VOLUMES

The liter is the unit that is used with the metric system to measure how much liquid something can hold. The symbol "ℓ" stands for liter.

Go to the Metric supply area and pick up a container labeled "ℓ liter." Fill the container with water and try to get an idea of how much 1 liter really is. Obtain at least four other containers of different sizes and shapes, and try to guess whether each would hold less than one liter, more than one liter, half a liter, two liters, three liters, etc. Then check your guesses by pouring the water from the liter-measure into each of the containers. Refill the container as needed. A liter is the amount of liquid that can be held in a container 1 dm by 1 dm by 1 dm (1 dm × 1 dm × 1 dm = 1 liter).

Container	Predict	Measure
1		
2		
3		
4		

Again, prefixes are used to show very large or very small quantities. Because most of the substances that you will be measuring are relatively small, you will need to learn about *milliliters*.

Pictured below is a centicube. A centicube measures 1 centimeter by 1 centimeter by 1 centimeter, so its volume is one cubic centimeter. If we filled this centicube with liquid, we would have *one milliliter* of liquid. Milliliter is symbolized ml.

 One milliliter is the capacity of a centicube (1 cm × 1 cm × 1 cm)

Any container that is graduated in milliliters can be used to measure small amounts of liquid.

Obtain a graduated cylinder from the supply area and pour some water into it. If the graduated cylinder is glass, you should notice that the upper surface of the water is curved or crescent-shaped. This curved surface is called the meniscus. When you measure the volume of a liquid, you should line up your eyes, as shown in the diagram, with the bottom of the meniscus. If you are using a plastic graduated cylinder, it will not have a meniscus. What volume is shown in the following diagram?

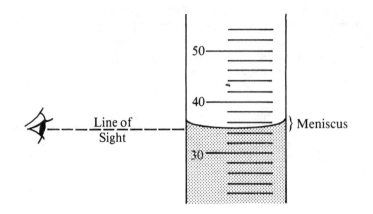

You should have read the volume as 35 ml.

As you have probably already learned, it is important to determine how many milliliters are represented by each mark on the graduated cylinder. It may differ from container to container. How much liquid is contained in each of the following graduated cylinders?

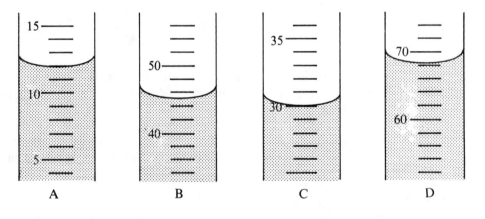

The answers are given below.

Self-check: a.   12 ml
b.   45 ml
c.   30 ml
d.   68 ml

More about measuring volume.

The basic unit of measure for the volume of solids or space is the *cubic meter*. Your kitchen stove probably measures about 1 meter by 1 meter by 1 meter, or 1 cubic meter.

The *cubic centimeter* is used to measure the volume of small solid objects. Cubic centimeters is symbolized cm^3.

Suppose you were asked to find the volume of a small rock. You would need to determine two things:

1.   What *units* will you use in your answer?
2.   What *process* will you use to do the measuring?

Since the object you are measuring here is solid and relatively small, the cubic centimeter is appropriate. If the rock is irregular in shape it would be impossible to measure its volume accurately with a ruler; but if you dropped the rock into a graduated cylinder of water, you would notice the water rising in the cylinder. If the water rose 4 ml, would the volume of the rock be 4 ml? Of course not, because our answer must be in cubic centimeters. We will have the right answer as soon as we find how a milliliter and a cubic centimeter compare. Do this simple activity to find out:

Use the centicubes to investigate to determine if 1 cubic centimeter is equal to 1 milliliter. (Remember a centicube is a cubic centimeter.) In the space below write the relationship between 1 cubic centimeter and 1 milliliter.

Now if you say that rock which displaced 4 ml of water has a volume of 4 cm³ you are right!

For practice . . .

From the supply area, obtain a baby food jar, five marbles, four washers, and a graduated cylinder. Find the following:

a.   amount of water that a baby food jar holds
b.   volume of five centicubes
c.   volume of five marbles
d.   volume of a block of wood, 2 cm by 4 cm by 6 cm
e.   volume of four washers

The answers are given below.

Self-check: The volumes are:

a.   baby food jar: 142 ml
b.   five centicubes: 5 cm³
c.   five marbles: 8 cm³
d.   block of wood 2 cm $\times$ 4 cm $\times$ 6 cm:
        48 cubic centimeters (perhaps you forgot, to obtain volumes of solid objects you multiply l $\times$ w $\times$ h)
e.   four washers: 2 cm³

Gather your thoughts about measuring metric volumes and fill in the following chart:

If you want to measure . . .	You should use a . . .	And measure in . . .
volume of relatively large amounts of a liquid (such as large cans of paint, tanks of gas, cartons of milk)		
volume of relatively small amounts of a liquid (as in tiny bottles of perfume, doses of cough medicine, small amounts called for in recipes)		
volume of relatively large solids or amounts of space (such as the volume of a load of lumber, or the volume of a room)		
volume of relatively small solids or amounts of space (such as the volume of a rock sample, or the volume of air in a small area)		

Compare your chart with the following one.

Self-check:

If you want to measure . . .	You should use a . . .	And measure in . . .
volume of relatively large amounts of a liquid (such as large cans of paint, tanks of gas, cartons of milk)	liter measure	liters (ℓ)
volume of relatively small amounts of a liquid (as in tiny bottles of perfume, doses of cough medicine, small amounts called for in recipes)	cylinder, beaker, or measurer graduated in milliliters	milliliters (ml)
volume of relatively large solids or amounts of space (such as the volume of a load of lumber, or the volume of a room)	meterstick or tape and measure length, height, width; $v = l \times h \times w$ or measure the amount of water the solid displaces	cubic meters (m^3)
volume of relatively small solids or amounts of space (such as the volume of a rock sample, or the volume of air in a small area)	graduated measurer and measure the amount of water the solid displaces or if possible, measure length, height, width; $v = l \times w \times h$	cubic centimeters (cm^3)

Activity 6

MEASURING METRIC TEMPERATURE

Temperature in the metric system is measured with a Celsius thermometer. Examine the Celsius thermometer pictured below. Observe the three standard temperatures marked on the scale: the temperature at which water boils (100 °C), the temperature at which water freezes (0 °C), and normal body temperature (37 °C).

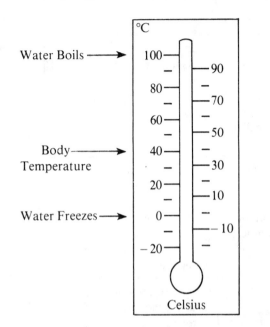

The symbol ° means degree. The temperature 20 °C, for example, should be read as twenty degrees Celsius.

Obtain a Celsius thermometer from the supply area. Examine the scale on the thermometer. Is the thermometer calibrated in one degree intervals? two degree intervals? five degree intervals? Measure the room temperature.

1. Number of degrees per interval on the scale _____
2. Room temperature is _____

Check your answers with someone else's.

In addition to the Celsius thermometer, obtain a baby food jar and some ice from the supply area. Fill the baby food jar half full of cold water. Measure the temperature of the water. Be sure to give the thermometer a few seconds to adjust before reading it. Add an ice cube to the water. Measure the temperature every two minutes while stirring the water gently. Complete the following table:

Time	Temperature
Temperature of water before adding ice	_____
Temperature of water after adding the ice	_____
After 2 minutes	_____
4 minutes	_____
6 minutes	_____
8 minutes	_____

Compare your answers with the ones that follow.

Self-check: Your table should be something like this:

Time	Temperature
Before adding ice	18 °C
After adding the ice:	
2 minutes	13 °C
4 minutes	12 °C
6 minutes	10 °C
8 minutes	10 °C

Don't be disturbed if your answers aren't the same as ours. A lot of factors can influence the results. The important thing is that you should be able to read the Celsius thermometer.

Optional Activity

**MEASURING
FORCES**

Whenever you measure a push or a pull, you are measuring force. The unit of force in the metric system is the *Newton* (N). Newtons are a measure of how much force is being exerted on an object.

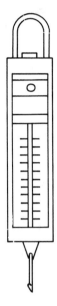

Instruments like the spring scale shown on the left and the personal scale are used to measure force. The spring scale may be hung, held, or laid on a flat surface. The greater the force being measured, the longer the spring is stretched.

A simple force measurer for measuring small forces could be made using a rubber band. Hang objects on the rubber band and calibrate the distance each stretches the band.

Weight is a force. It is the pull of gravity on nearby objects. The earth's gravitational pull on nearby objects is stronger than the moon's gravitational pull on objects near its surface. A person would weigh about one-sixth of his earth weight on the moon.

Keep in mind that mass is the measure of the amount of matter in an object. Therefore, the mass of an object would remain the same no matter where in the universe it is placed.

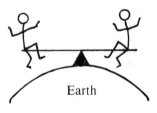

Earth

Moon

Two children balancing one another on a teeter-totter on earth, would still balance one another on the moon. Each child's *mass* would be the same on the moon as on earth, but each child would *weigh* about one-sixth as much on the moon as on earth.

If we keep our thoughts earth bound, we can state a definite relationship between mass and weight. At sea level, on the earth's surface, a kilogram mass weighs about 10 newtons.

Continue on and take the mastery test on the next page.

Metric Measures Mastery Test

I. In the spaces provided, write the most appropriate metric unit in which each of the following should be measured:

1. The length of a football field should be measured in _____

   _____ .

2. The temperature of the room should be measured in _____

   _____ .

3. The volume of a marble should be measured in _____ .

4. The diameter of a straw should be measured in _____ .

5. The mass of a football player should be measured in _____

   _____ .

6. The width of a T.V. screen should be measured in _____

   _____ .

7. The amount of water used in a baking recipe should be measured in

   _____ .

8. The amount of gas an automobile gas tank can hold should be measured in

   _____ .

9. The mass of a package of chewing gum should be measured in _____

   _____ .

10. The mass of a postage stamp should be measured in _____

    _____ .

II. Use what you know about metric prefixes and state equivalent metric measures for each of the following:

1. 1 meter = _____ decimeters

2. 1 dm = _____ cm = _____ mm

3. 1 mm = _____ m = _____ dm = _____ cm

4. 2 kilometers = _____ meters

5. 4000 m = _____ km

6. 500 meters = _____ hectometers

7. 1 km = _____ dam

8. 1 km = _____ hm

9. 1 liter = _____ milliliters

III. Take a "Measurement Test Packet" from the supply area and—
1. Measure the length and width of the packet envelope to the nearest 0.5 centimeters.
2. Remove a toothpick from the envelope and measure its length to the nearest millimeter.
3. Remove the string of washers from the envelope and measure its mass (weight) to the nearest gram.
4. Find the volume of the string of washers.
5. Record the present room temperature in degrees Celsius.
6. Measure the length of the line drawn below. Give your answer in millimeters, centimeters, decimenters, and meters.

_____

The answers to the mastery test follow.

Answers for Mastery Test:

I. 1. length of football field—meters (m)
    2. temperature of room—degrees Celsius (°C)
    3. volume of a marble—cubic centimeters (cm³)
    4. diameter of a straw—millimeters (mm)
    5. mass (weight) of a football player—kilograms (kg)
    6. width of a T.V. screen—centimeters (cm)
    7. amount of water used in a recipe—milliliters (ml)
    8. amount of gas a tank can hold—liters (ℓ)
    9. mass (weight) of a package of gum—grams (g)
    10. mass (weight) of a postage stamp—milligrams (mg)

II. 1. 1 meter = 10 decimeters
     2. 1 dm = 10 cm = 100 mm
     3. 1 mm   1/1000 m = 1/100 dm = 1/10 cm
     4. 2 kilometers = 2000 meters
     5. 4000 m = 4 km
     6. 500 meters = 5 hectometers
     7. 1 km = 100 dam
     8. 1 km = 10 hm
     9. 1 liter = 1000 milliliters

III. 1-5. Check your answers with those given on the card in the "Measurement Test Packet."
     6. length of line: 115 mm, 11.5 cm, 1.15 dm, .115 m

Ideas for Your Classroom

Measuring for the sake of measuring is dull and pointless, so incorporate measuring with other class activities. Here are some suggestions which you can expand with your own ideas. The activities you choose should depend a great deal on your students' interests.

1. Construct other measuring instruments from the ones already available in the classroom. What would you need to measure the distance between the office and the cafeteria? The distance around your waist? The distance from the second story window to the ground?

2. Measure growing plants. Keep a record and make comparisons between plants grown in different conditions.

3. Construct a map of the classroom representing actual distances.
4. Measure shadows at different times of the day.
5. Keep a record of the amount of food and water a classroom pet requires each day.
6. Here is a (metric) recipe for growing crystals. The results are fascinating!

   5 ml household ammonia
   15 ml water
   15 ml table salt
   15 ml bluing

   Mix together and pour over rocks, sand, sponges, wood, or bits of brick and cement. Spread out on a metal tray. Let it stand and watch the crystals grow.
7. Make bread, cookies, or pudding. Measure the ingredients, temperature, and time.

The ESS unit called *Match and Measure* has some excellent ideas for getting your students actively involved in some worthwhile measuring activities.

PREDICTION 5

To do the Prediction activities that follow you will need:

—a pendulum support (nothing special, even a desk will do)
—a string or cord
—2 pendulum bobs (sinkers, washers, or any other small weights)
—a containter of buttons (25 red, 10 blue, 10 green, and 5 white)
—a meter stick

For the optional activity you will need:

—a glass jar (a liter or larger)
—enough particles to fill the jar (peas, marbles, rice, etc.)

WHY PREDICTION IS IMPORTANT

A prediction is a forecast of what a future observation might be. The ability to construct dependable predictions about objects and events allows us to determine appropriate behavior toward our environment. Predicting is closely related to observing, inferring, and classifying—an excellent example of a skill in one process being dependent on the skills acquired in other processes. Prediction is based on careful observation and the inferences made about relationships between observed events. Remember that inferences are explanations or intrepretations of observations and that inferences are supported by observations. Classification is employed when we identify observed similarities or differences to impart order to objects and events. Order in our environment permits us to recognize patterns and to predict from the patterns what future observations will be.

Children need to learn to ask such questions as "If this happens, what will follow?" "What will happen if I do this?" As teachers we need to be very careful about the kinds of predictions we make about student behavior and performance.

Goals:

In these exercises you will learn to construct predictions based on patterns of observed evidence and to test your predictions for dependability.

Performance Objectives:

After completing this set of activities you should be able to:

1. distinguish among observation, inference, and prediction.
2. construct predictions based on observed patterns of evidence.
3. construct tests for predictions.

Activity 1

DISTINGUISHING AMONG OBSERVATION, INFERENCE, AND PREDICTION

The following brief definitions may help you to remember in distinguishing among observation, inference, and prediction. (See the separate learning activities for thorough treatment of each process skill.)

Information gained through the senses: *Observation*
Why it happened: *Inference*
What I expect to observe: *Prediction*

The following activity is intended to give you practice in distinguishing among these important processes. Read the first two frames of the cartoon and the statements that follow. Indicate whether each statement is an observation, inference, or prediction. (Take the point of view of the cartoon characters.)

B. C. by permission of Johnny Hart and Field Enterprises, Inc.

1. "In about 2 minutes that mountain is going to blow sky-high."
   _____

2. "I can feel the rumbling (earth vibrating) beneath my feet."
   _____

3. The "rumbling" is caused by the volcano. _____

Was Peter's prediction based on careful and comprehensive observation? How much *confidence* do you have in his prediction? To see how the cartoon turns out, look below.

Self-check: Compare your answers with someone else's or check your answers with those below.

1. <u>Prediction</u> (A forecast of what a future observation will be.)
2. <u>Observation</u> (Information gained through the senses.)
3. <u>Inference</u> (An explanation for the observation.)

B. C. by permission of Johnny Hart and Field Enterprises, Inc.

Activity 2

CONSTRUCTING PREDICTIONS BASED ON OBSERVED PATTERNS

Date	Sunrise Time	Date	Sunrise Time
January 1	7:24	May 1	5:00
January 15	7:20	June 1	4:31
February 1	7:12	July 1	4:33
February 15	6:52	August 1	4:56
March 1	6:35	September 1	5:25
March 15	6:08	October 1	5:54
April 1	5:42	November 1	6:28
April 15	5:21	December 1	7:01

The table at the left shows the times the sun was observed to rise (at a specific latitude) at different times of the year.

But, what about days in the year *not* shown in the table? Would it be possible to *predict* sunrise times for those days not directly observed? Let's see . . .

We make predictions by first looking for patterns. Answer the following questions designed to help you find a pattern in the observed sunrise times:

1. What time did the sun rise on Jan. 1? _____ On Feb. 1? _____
2. Would you expect sunrise time for Jan. 15 to be about halfway between sunrise times for Jan. 1 and Feb. 1? _____ Is it? _____ (Check the observed time.)
   (Jan. 15 is not exactly *half*way between Jan. 1 and Feb. 1; it is instead 14/31 of the way—14 days between Jan. 1 and Jan. 15 and 31 days between Jan. 1 and Feb. 1—but it's close enough.)
3. Use the "halfway" method to predict the sunrise time for Feb. 15. (Try not to look until you've figured it.) What is your prediction? _____ Then check your prediction with the observed sunrise time in the table.
   Check: There is a difference of 37 minutes between 7:12 on Feb. 1 and 6:35 on March 1. Half the difference, about 19 minutes, subtracted from the Feb. 1 sunrise time gives a prediction of 6:53 for Feb. 15.

Try this one . . . Predict sunrise time for October 15. Then check your answer in the self-check.

B. C. by permission of Johnny Hart and Field Enterprises, Inc.

Self-check: If you used the "halfway" method to find the predicted sunrise time for October 15, your calculations probably look something like this:

```
  November 1   6:28
− October 1    5:54
              34 minutes difference
```

Half of 34 minutes is 17 minutes.

```
October 1      5:54
       +         17
              6:11 Predicted sunrise time
```

If you used the more exact method of calculating, your figures might look like this:

```
  November     6:28
− October      5:54
              34 minutes difference
```
14/31 of 34 minutes is about 15 minutes.

```
October 1      5:54
       +         15
              6:09 predicted sunrise time
```

4. Suppose you wanted to predict a sunrise time for a date that was not halfway between two other given dates? Using the table, determine the sunrise time for September 10.

Self-check: September 10 is about one-third the way between September 1 and October 1.

```
  October 1   5:54
− September 1  5:25
              29 minutes difference
```

10/30 or 1/3 of 29 minutes is about 10 minutes.

```
September 1  5:25
       +        10
              5:35 Predicted sunrise time for September 10.
```

Activity 3

PRACTICE IN MAKING PREDICTIONS

When making predictions it is important to:

a. collect data through careful observation.
b. search for patterns of events (classify).
c. infer cause-effect relationships.
d. construct a statement about what you think a future observation will be, based on the pattern of events (predict).
e. test the dependability of the prediction.

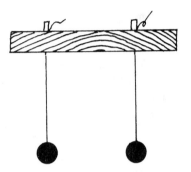

This next activity involves the use of pendulums. (With pendulums your students can have fun and learn important concepts at the same time! See the ESS unit "Pendulums" for many activities providing for investigation and keeping interest high.) Go to the prediction supply area, pick up a pendulum support, and set up your pendulums like those shown.

Set one of the pendulums in motion and begin exploring "round-trips." A pendulum makes a "round trip" when it is set in motion and returns to its starting position.

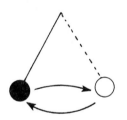

In your explorations, try to find out what it is that affects the length of time it takes to make a round trip. Check the things in this list which you feel affect the round-trip time:

1. _____ the size of the bob

2. _____ the mass of the bob

3. _____ the distance of the swing

4. _____ the length of the pendulum

5. _____ the type of path (back and forth, circle, etc.)

Compare your answers with someone else's or check your answers with those below.

Self-check:

You probably found that the round-trip time of a pendulum is *most* affected by the *length* of the pendulum.

Activity 4

While you were exploring with pendulums, you were making observations and gathering data about pendulums and motion. Through exploration and observation you began making inferences as to what might affect round-trip time for the pendulum. In the next activity you will concentrate on one feature, the length of the pendulum, and begin searching for *patterns*. Discovering patterns will enable you to make dependable predictions about the behavior of pendulums. By improving your inferences about what affects a pendulum's swing you increase the likelihood that your predictions are correct. In other words, you are building *confidence* in your predictions.

You may also increase the amount of confidence you have in a prediction by arriving at the same predicted values by different methods. The closer the agreement between predicted values arrived at by different methods, the greater the confidence you may have in the prediction.

In this next activity you will observe what happens when the length of a pendulum is systematically changed. Your observations will then be a basis for making predictions about the motion of the pendulum. Follow directions carefully.

Step 1: In this part of the activity you will be working with columns 1 and 2 of the chart that follows. Adjust the length of the pendulum to 15 cm (measure to the middle of the bob). Count the number of full swings in a 30 second interval. Record the number of full swings in the blank space in column 2.

Repeat the procedure for *25* cm, *35* cm, and *45* cm. These are the observed number of full swings for those pendulum lengths.

(1) Length (cm)	(2) Observed Swings	(3) Predicted by Method 1	(4) Predicted by Method 2	(5) Observed Swings
15				
20				
25				
30				
35				
40				
45				

Step 2: Examine columns 1 and 2. *Without swinging the pendulum,* predict the number of swings the pendulum would make in a 30 second interval for 20 cm, 30 cm, and 40 cm. Enter these predictions in the blank spaces in column 3. These represent your predictions using method 1 (as used in Activity 2).

There is more than one way to make predictions using this data. This brings us to the next method—graphing.

Step 3: Using the data from columns 1 and 2, plot the data from columns 1 and 2 for 15 cm, 25 cm, 35 cm, and 45 cm, and, on the following graph, draw a smooth curve through the plotted points.

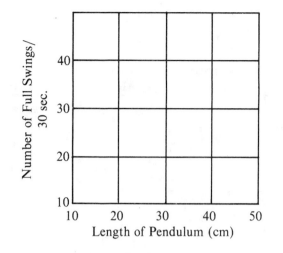

Compare your graph with the one below.

Self-check: Your graph probably looks something like this:

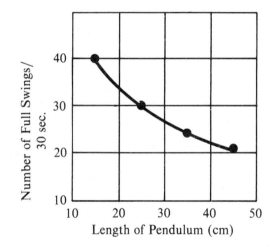

Step 4: By reading the graph, predict the number of swings for 20 cm, 30 cm, 40 cm. Enter these predictions in the table under Column 4. These represent your predictions by Method 2—Graphing.

Compare the values you predicted by Method 1 with those predicted by Method 2. The closer the agreement between the predicted values obtained by different methods, the greater the confidence you should have in your prediction. How confident are you that your predicted values are correct?

Step 5: Put the predictions to the test by observing the number of full swings of the pendulum at 20 cm, 30 cm, and 40 cm. Enter these numbers in the table under column 5. These are your observed values. Compare these to your predicted values. They should be fairly close.

Self-check: Your table may look something like this:

(1) Length (cm)	(2) Observed Swings	(3) Predicted by Method 1	(4) Predicted by Method 2	(5) Observed Swings
15	40			
20		35	35	34
25	30			
30		27	27	27
35	25			
40		23	23	23
45	21			

Activity 5

**PREDICTION
AND CHANCE**

Few things are as dependable as sunrise time and the period of a pendulum . . . not even the weather. Many factors can affect the accuracy of a prediction and often that is chance.

To illustrate this point, you will need the container of buttons. First, count the buttons to make sure that there are 25 red, 10 blue, 10 green, and 5 white ones. Because all the buttons are alike except for color, each button has the same chance to be taken as any other button (if taken without looking). Suppose you were to take a large sample (half of all the buttons) from the container, how many of each color would you predict?

Red   = _____

Blue   = _____

Green   = _____

White   = _____

Self-check:

Red   = 12 or 13
Blue   = 5
Green   = 5
White   = 2 or 3

The reason for the 12 or 13 and the 2 or 3 is that there are no half buttons in the container.

Why not try it out? Take half the buttons from the container and see how they compare with your predictions.

Red   = _____

Blue   = _____

Green   = _____

White   = _____

Self-check:

Compare your answers with someone else's. While they will vary, they probably are fairly close.

Often it is impossible to take a very large sample like half of the entire population because the population is very large and perhaps scattered over a very large area. Think how difficult it would be to observe the numbers of all the different kinds of plants in Yellowstone Park. What biologists do in situations such as this is to take many small samples.

Suppose you were to take a small sample of ten buttons from the container. Ten buttons is one fifth of all the buttons. How many red, blue, green, and white buttons would you predict to be in the sample? Enter the numbers in the table below beside Predicted Results.

	Red	Blue	Green	White
Predicted Results				
Your Sample				

Now take ten buttons from the container and enter the numbers of red, blue, green, and white buttons beside Your Sample. Compare your answers with the Self-check or someone else's.

Self-check:

	Red	Blue	Green	White
Predicted Results	5	2	2	1
Our Results	3	4	2	1

Your answers will probably differ from our results and everyone else's.

If the predicted numbers were close to what you observed in your sample, you are probably satisfied with your accuracy and your "confidence" is high. If your prediction was not close to what you observed in your sample, you are probably tempted to try it again. The reason for the difference is that chance played a part in which buttons were selected in the sample.

Does the number of samples affect the accuracy of a prediction? Lets find out. In this activity, you will take five separate samples and see how closely the results compare with the predicted results.

1. Without looking, reach into the container and take a sample of ten buttons.
2. Record the number of red, blue, green, and white buttons under column labeled Sample 1.
3. Return the buttons to the container and mix them with the other buttons.
4. Repeat the procedure until you have completed all five samples.

Buttons	Sample 1	Sample 2	Sample 3	Sample 4	Sample 5	Total of Samples	Total Population
Red							25
Blue							10
Green							10
White							5

Each of the five individual samples probably differed from the predicted amounts as much as the first activity. Now total the number of red buttons taken in all five samples and record that number under total of samples for red. Repeat this process for the blue, green, and white samples.

How close were your total samples to predicting the total population of buttons? Compare your answer with ours in the Self-check.

Self-check:
(Our Results)

Buttons	Sample 1	Sample 2	Sample 3	Sample 4	Sample 5	Total of Samples	Total Population
Red	6	4	6	6	3	25	25
Blue	4	3	2	1	5	15	10
Green	0	0	2	2	2	6	10
White	0	3	0	1	0	4	5

Were your answers closer, farther from, or about the same in predicting the correct amounts of red, green, blue, and white buttons?

Why did our answers differ? What do you suppose would happen to the accuracy of your prediction if you took ten samples instead of five?

Optional Activities for Prediction: Estimating Large Quantities

Have you ever wondered. . . .

— How many blades of grass are in a lawn?
— How many words are in a book?
— How many grains of sand are in a beach?
— How many leaves are in a tree?
— How do they know how many eagles are alive?
— How many words are in a newspaper?
— How many stars are in the sky?
— How many grains of rice are in a bag?
— How many flakes are in a box of cereal?
— How many jelly beans are in that jar so you could win a bike?

As you can see, sometimes it is more practical to use estimates rather than actually counting. As a test for your ingenuity, devise and execute a method to determine the number of particles in a jar. The jar could be a liter of marbles, a jar of buttons, a jar of rice, or anything else your instructor is devious enough to contrive.

Compare your plans with those in the Self-check, your instructor's, or someone else's.

Self-check:

Listed below are some methods that may be used to predict large numbers of things. If you discover other methods, add them to the list.

1. *Taking a Sample:* Multiply the number of particles in a small sample by the number of sample-size quantities in the total.
2. *Counting by Area and Volume:* Measure out a cupful of 250 ml; push the particles into a square; count the particles along one edge and square this number to get the number of particles the container held. Measure the number of containers held by the total sample and multiply this number by the number of particles per container.
3. *Weighing:* Find the weight of a small, easy to count, quantity and compare it to the weight of the whole.
4. *Halving or Doubling:* Divide the total quantity into two parts. Continue halving until you have a small enough quantity to count. Then double the number as many times as you halved the amount of particles.

Prediction Mastery Test

Below is a graph showing the average monthly high temperatures for a particular city. Examine the graph and answer the questions that follow.

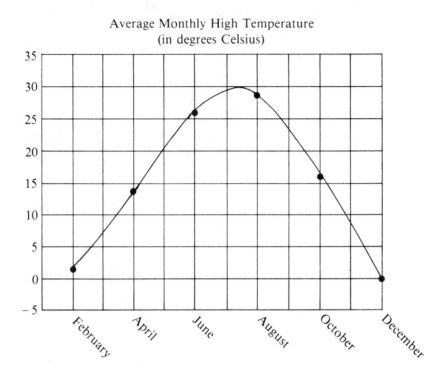

Average Monthly High Temperature
(in degrees Celsius)

1. Through what basic process skill was the information in the graph first gathered?

_____

2. Through what basic process skill was the information in the graph organized and put

into order? _____

3. Through what basic process skill would you attempt to explain why the curve on the

graph takes on this particular shape? _____

4. What was the average high temperature recorded for the month of February?

_____ April? _____

5. Through what process would you forecast what the average high temperature would be

for the month of May? _____

6. Predict the average high temperature for the month of March: _____ January:

_____

7. Where in the United States would you predict this city might be located:

_____

8. Write a statement comparing the amount of *confidence* you have in your predictions in item #6 with the confidence you have in your prediction in item #7.

9. Kim had a jar containing 100 pennies. Twenty-five of the pennies were dated 1983, fifty of the pennies were dated 1984 and the remaining pennies were dated 1985. Without looking, Kim took ten pennies from the jar and examined their dates. How many pennies would you predict that she found for each of the years?

1983 = _____ pennies

1984 = _____ pennies

1985 = _____ pennies

10. When Kim looked at the pennies, she found that five pennies were dated 1983, four pennies were dated 1984 and one penny was dated 1985. If Kim were to obtain a more accurate idea as to the distribution of pennies for 1983, 1984, and 1985, what two things could she do?

_____

_____

Compare your answers with those in the self-check.

Self-check:
1. Observation
2. Classification
3. Inference
4. about 2°C, about 14°C
5. Prediction
6. About 8°; about 1°C
7. The city was actually Detroit, Michigan
8. You should have felt much more confident in the predictions you made in item #6 than the prediction you made for item #7. The difference lies in the fact that your predictions for #6 were based upon careful and comprehensive observations and a definite pattern appears in the data. Your prediction for item #7 was most likely a guess.
9. Answers will vary somewhat, but with luck you could expect two or three dated 1983, five dated 1984, and two or three dated 1985.
10. Kim could take either a larger sample like half of the pennies or take many small samples of the pennies.

Ideas for Your Classroom

1. *Food Webs.* Here is a simple food web:

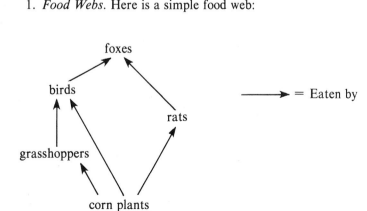

Predict what would happen if any one organism were removed from the web.

2. *Electromagnetism.* Construct an electromagnet by wrapping about ten coils of electrical wire around a nail and connecting the ends of the wire to the opposite ends of a flashlight battery. Count the number of paperclips the electromagnet can pick up. Predict ways to increase the strength of the electromagnet.

3. *Inclined Planes.* Make an incline by placing a book under one end of a ruler. Place a marble in the groove of the ruler at the top of the incline. Release the marble and measure the distance the marble travels. Predict how the distance the marble travels can be increased.

4. *Electrical Conductors and Insulators.* Construct an electrical circuit by connecting the opposite ends of a flashlight battery to a flashlight bulb using two wires. Be sure the circuit works (the bulb lights). Test various objects to see if they are good conductors of electricity by first making a gap in the circuit between the bulb and one wire and inserting the object to be tested in the gap. If the bulb lights the object is a conductor. With a new set of objects made of various materials (glass, rubber, plastic, wood, different kinds of metals) predict which ones are conductors.

5. *Sound.* Add different amounts of water to several pop bottles and predict which will produce the highest pitch when struck sharply with a pencil. Which will give the highest pitch when someone blows into the top of the bottle?

6. *Combustion.* Invert jars of varying volumes over burning birthday candles. Predict which candle will burn the longest.

7. *Sound.* Hammer nails in pairs at various distances apart on a board. Stretch a rubber band over each pair of nails. Predict which rubber band will make the highest pitch when plucked. Predict a way to change the pattern.

INFERENCE 6

To do the inference activities you will need:

—an inference board
—a circuit tester (battery, three wires, bulb)
—a mystery box

WHY INFERENCE IS IMPORTANT

We have a better appreciation of our environment when we are able to interpret and explain things happening around us. We learn to recognize patterns and expect these patterns to reoccur under the same conditions. Much of our own behavior is based on the inferences we make about events. Scientists form hypotheses based on the inferences they make regarding investigations. As teachers we constantly make inferences about why our students behave as they do. Learning itself is an inference made from observed changes in learner behavior.

Goals:

In these exercises you will learn about model building and develop skills necessary to make proper inferences based on observation.

Performance Objectives:

After completing this set of activities you should be able to:

1. given an object or event construct a set of inferences from your observations about that object or event.
2. given additional observations about the object or event, identify the inferences that should be accepted, modified, or rejected.

Activity 1

**CONSTRUCTING
INFERENCES FROM
OBSERVATIONS**

While an observation is an experience perceived through one or more of the senses, an inference is *an explanation or interpretation of an observation.* Suppose, for example, you observe a middle-aged neighbor shoveling very heavy snow from his drive; suddenly he stiffens, grasps his chest, and falls to the ground. One inference you might make is that he is having a heart attack. You might base this inference on some knowledge you have about heart attacks as well as on the behavior you have witnessed. The fact that you have made this inference, and then acted accordingly, may be extremely important.

An inference, then, is a statement that goes beyond the evidence and attempts to interpret or explain a set of observations. It follows that every inference must be based on direct observation. Look at the comic strip and the set of statements about the strip below. As you read the statements try to determine which are observations and which are inferences.

B. C. by permission of Johnny Hart and Field Enterprises, Inc.

1. The ant has two antennae.

2. The ant can read.

3. The ant is worried.

4. The ant is perspiring.

5. The ant is under the sign.

Statement number 1 is an observation perceived through the sense of sight. You can see and count the number of antennae. All the other statements are intrepretations of what you observe. They are inferences. You can only infer that the ant is able to read the sign, that those little drops above the ant's head are perspiration, that he is worried about the situation, or that he is under the sign.

Look at the comic strip and set of statements that follow. Identify each statement as an observation or inference in the space provided.

B. C. by permission of Johnny Hart and Field Enterprises, Inc.

_____ 1. Peter has a whistle.

_____ 2. Peter blows the whistle.

_____ 3. B.C. doesn't hear the whistle.

_____ 4. The anteater hears the whistle.

_____ 5. The anteater doesn't like the whistle.

_____ 6. Peter and B.C. think the whistle doesn't work.

Compare your answers with someone else's or check your answers with the Self-check.

Self-check: Based on the information given you in the cartoon the statements could be identified as follows:

1. Peter has a whistle. <u>observation</u>

   The object not only looks like a whistle but Peter tells us that it is a whistle. The fact that it is a whistle is not left to our interpretation.

2. Peter blows the whistle. <u>inference</u>

   We cannot hear the whistle. From the look on Peter's face and the squiggly lines drawn above the whistle, we can only infer that the whistle is being blown.

3. B.C. doesn't hear the whistle. <u>observation</u>

   We can accept this as an observation because B.C. tells us he doesn't hear a thing. The fact that he does not hear the whistle is not left to our interpretation.

4. The anteater hears the whistle. <u>inference</u>

   We can observe that the anteater's body is out of shape and wrinkled and from this observation we can infer that the anteater hears the whistle.

5. The anteater doesn't like the whistle. <u>inference</u>

   From our observation of the anteater's appearance we can only infer that he doesn't like the whistle.

6. Peter and B. C. think the whistle doesn't work. <u>inference</u>

   This is an interpretation based on the fact that we observe Peter and B.C. throwing the whistle away. Interpretations are inferences.

Activity 2

FORMULATING INFERENCES FROM OBSERVATIONS

This next activity is designed to help you learn to formulate inferences. Every inference must be drawn from an observation, so you will first be making careful observations and then you will be interpreting or explaining those observations. These interpretations or explanations of observations are inferences. (This is also a neat activity as an exercise in inferential thinking in creative writing!)

Observe these "tracks in the snow". To help you think more logically about the picture, it has been separated into frames. Make at least two observations about each frame, and for each observation write at least one inference that could be drawn from that observation. (More than one inference can be drawn from one observation.)

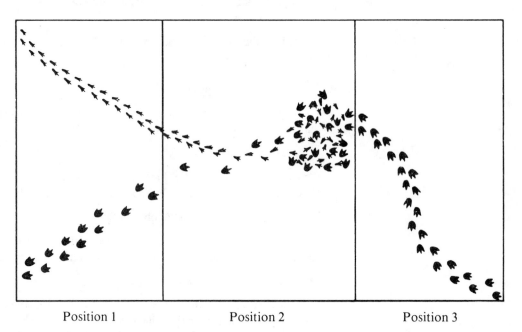

| Position 1 | Position 2 | Position 3 |

American Geological Institute, INVESTIGATING THE EARTH, Fourth Edition, Copyright © 1984 by Houghton Mifflin Company. Used with permission.

	Observations	**Inferences**
Position 1	1. Example: Large footprints get farther apart.	a. The animal is stepping over stones. b. The animal is running.
	2. _____	
	3. _____	
	4. _____	
Position 2	1. _____	
	2. _____	
	3. _____	

Position 3   1. _____

            2. _____

            3. _____

Check your inferences with someone else's or with those listed in the Self-check.

Self-check: Here are just a few inferences you might have made. There could be many, many more. In checking your inferences be certain that each is based on a specific observation. More than one inference can be drawn from a single observation.

	Observations	**Inferences**
Position 1	1. One set of prints is smaller than the other.	1. One animal is smaller than the other.
	2. The small and large prints are headed in the same direction.	2. Both are walking toward something.
	3. There are three toes for each print.	3. Both animals are birds.
	4. The small and large prints get closer to each other.	4. a. The large animal is pursuing the small animal. b. Both are walking in a gulley.
	5. The larger prints get farther apart.	5. a. The larger bird is going downhill. b. The larger bird is running. c. The larger bird is stepping over stones.
Position 2	1. The prints converge.	1. a. The larger animal catches and either eats or carries off the smaller animal. b. The animals were there at different times. c. Both animals discovered food in the same place.
	2. The prints become all mixed up.	2. a. The animals were milling about. b. The animals were fighting.
	3. The smaller footprints get farther apart.	3. The smaller animal begins to run.
Position 3	1. The small tracks stop.	1. a. The larger animal ate the smaller one. b. The smaller animal flew away. c. The snow at this point became crusty and the smaller animal was not heavy enough to make tracks.
	2. The large prints are close together.	2. The larger animal was walking rather than running.

Activity 3

This activity will give you practice and confidence in making inferences and in addition, it will help you to learn to re-evaluate your inferences as new data is introduced. You'll be using two pieces of equipment, an inference board and a circuit tester.

Circuit Tester   Inference Board

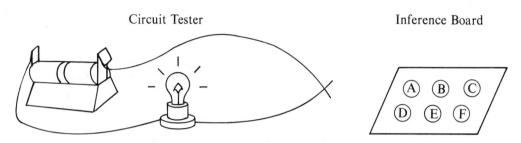

Go the supply area and pick up an inference board and a circuit tester. Make sure the circuit tester is assembled like the one pictured above. When the bare metal ends of the wires are touched together, the bulb should light. If your bulb lights, you're right on target and doing fine. If your bulb does not light, check to see that the connections are good and the battery and light bulb are tight in their holders. Ask for help if you need it but be sure the tester works before going on.

The wires of your circuit tester form a pathway from the battery to the bulb and back to the battery again. Experiment and find out what happens when you disrupt, or break, this circuit by disconnecting the wires at any point.

Now examine the inference board. It is simply two pieces of cardboard, one of which has brass fasteners attached to it. When the cardboards are placed back to back only the heads of the fasteners are visible. Hidden between the cardboards are wires that connect some of the fasteners. Since you cannot observe the wires, you do not know how they are arranged.

You can use your circuit tester to learn more about the wiring pattern hidden within the inference board. Hook the tester up to the inference board as shown below. STOP!!! DO NOT TEST FOR ANY OTHER PATHWAYS.

Any statements you make about the pattern of wires within the inference board are inferences, not observations. You could observe the wires only by tearing the board open and looking at them. You can, however, observe that the bulb of the circuit tester either does or does not light when certain connections are made with the inference board. Based on these observations you can infer that the wires are arranged in a certain way to explain what you observe.

If you observe that the bulb does not light when the circuit tester is attached to **A** and **B**, then you may infer that there is no wire within the board that connects **A** and **B.** If, however, you observe that the bulb does light, then you may infer that **A** and **B** are somehow connected. **A** and **B** may be wired directly like this:

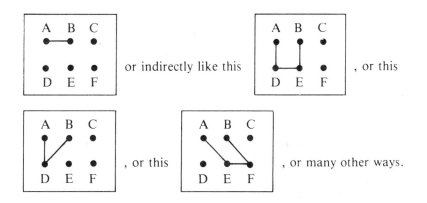

As long as there is some kind of a wire pathway between **A** and **B** the circuit tester bulb will light when connected to **A** and **B.**

Check your understanding at this point by doing this: Based on the observation that the bulb of the circuit tester does not light when connected to **A** and **B** of the inference board, draw at least three more possible wiring patterns, other than the ones shown above, that would explain what you observe. Check your answers with those in the self-check.

A	B	C		A	B	C		A	B	C
0	0	0		0	0	0		0	0	0
0	0	0		0	0	0		0	0	0
D	E	F		D	E	F		D	E	F

Self-check: Any drawing showing **A** and **B** connected indirectly by wires would be acceptable. Here are a few:

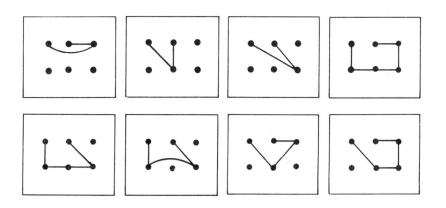

All of these patterns would explain the fact that the bulb lit when the circuit tester was connected to **A** and **B.** Keep going . . . your inference board is about to get more interesting.

At this point you have inferred something about the secret wiring pattern within the inference board by testing **A** and **B.** You can learn more about the board by doing some more testing. Use the circuit tester to answer these questions: Are A and C connected? Are A and

D connected? C and F? What other possible connections can you infer? Learn as much about your inference board as you can by testing all the possible combinations. In the chart below, indicate whether the bulb lights (+) or fails to light (−) for each combination.

Combination TESTED	AB	AC	AD	AE	AF	BC	BD	BE	BF	CD	CE	CF	DE	DF	EF
Response of bulb (+ or −)															

Compare your responses with someone else's or check your answers with those in the Self-check.

Self-check: Your chart should look like this:

Combination TESTED	AB	AC	AD	AE	AF	BC	BD	BE	BF	CD	CE	CF	DE	DF	EF
Response of bulb (+ or −)	+	−	+	−	+	−	+	−	+	−	−	−	−	+	−

From the observations you have recorded in the chart above you can make inferences about the possible pattern of wires within your inference board. Examine the pattern of wires shown below. Could this be a possible wiring pattern of your inference board?

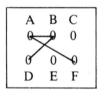

Check your answers with the Self-check.

Self-check: This wiring pattern does explain the observation that the combinations AB, AD, AF, BD, BF, and DF light the bulb. That this is *the* wiring pattern within the inference board is only an inference.

Could other wiring patterns explain the same observations recorded in your chart? On the following inference boards draw some more inferred wiring patterns, each of which might explain the observations in the chart above.

```
 A   B   C        A   B   C        A   B   C
 0   0   0        0   0   0        0   0   0

 0   0   0        0   0   0        0   0   0
 D   E   F        D   E   F        D   E   F
```

Compare your possible wiring patterns with those in the Self-check.

Self-check: There are many possible wiring patterns which could explain these observations, so be sure to compare your inferred pattern with someone else's. Some patterns you might have had are shown here.

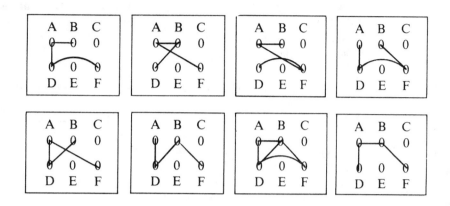

By now you have learned that many inferences can be drawn from the same set of observations. Which of your inferred wiring patterns is the actual wiring pattern within the inference board? The fact is that from the information given, it is not possible for you to infer the actual pattern. If, however, you were given more information about your actual circuit board, you would be able to re-examine your original set of inferences and determine which ones should be accepted, rejected, and modified. Let's try it.

Add the following bits of information about your actual inference board to the original set of observations you have already recorded in your chart.

1. No wires cross.
2. There are only three wires.
3. No more than two wires converge at any point.

With this new information about your inference board, re-examine your original set of inferences. Accept, reject, or modify the pattern you have already drawn. Now is it possible for you to infer the actual wiring pattern of your inference board? Draw the inferred pattern(s) below.

A B C	A B C	A B C
0 0 0	0 0 0	0 0 0
0 0 0	0 0 0	0 0 0
D E F	D E F	D E F

Compare your inferences with someone else's or check your pattern(s) with those that follow.

Self-check: The additional information given to you should have helped you to decide which of your original inferred patterns should be accepted, which should be rejected, and which should be modified. Actually, even with the new information, it is not possible to infer *the actual* pattern of wires within the inference board. Three possible patterns are shown here:

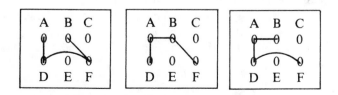

Inference Mastery Test

Go to the inference supply area and pick up a mystery box. Do not open the box or in any way tamper directly with the contents. Make at least five inferences about the contents of the box and identify the specific observation on which you base each inference. You may tilt, shake, roll, or rattle the box but do not peek inside. List your inferences and observations in the chart below.

Inferences   **Observations**

1. _____

2. _____

3. _____

4. _____

5. _____

Now open one end of the box and without looking inside put your hand in the box and gather some additional information about the contents. In the chart below, accept, reject, or modify each of your original inferences on the basis of this new information. Identify the observations on which you accept, reject, or modify each inference.

Inferences   **Observations**

1. _____

2. _____

3. _____

4. _____

5. _____

Compare your observations and inferences with your partner's or check your answers with those in the envelope taped to the mystery box.

Ideas for Your Classroom

1. *Pictures* are excellent for use in developing skills of observation and inference. Use pictures showing action that has already taken place and have students make observations and inferences about their observations. Comic strips, cartoons, coloring books, and comic books are good sources of pictures. Pictures of animals are also excellent for developing observation and inference skills. Organisms are adapted for their survival (e.g. coloration for protection, feet adapted for catching prey, feet for escaping predators, spines on cacti for protection, color to attract animals to eat the fruit like grapes, etc.).

2. *Mystery Boxes* are fun and intriguing as well as excellent activities for observation and inference making. Enclose unknown objects in a shoebox and have the students make as many observations as possible without opening the box. Try to involve as many senses as you can except sight, by providing the means to the student to feel or smell the object. Give students practice in accepting, modifying or rejecting inferences on the basis of additional information. Some objects that could be used include: a sugar cube, bar of

soap, a toothbrush, pine cone, popcorn, lemon, onion, or a stick of gum. There are many other objects that could be used.

3. *Unknown Gases* may be best done as demonstrations but students can participate and these exercises are wonderful for having students make inferences.

Oxygen

First you'll need:

—a glass jar or clear plastic container
—enough 3% hydrogen peroxide to fill the jar about half full.
—a cake or packet of yeast
—a candle (or splint) and matches

a. Fill the jar about half full with hydrogen peroxide and sprinkle some yeast into the peroxide. Have students record their observations. (What they *don't* see, smell, taste, feel, or hear can be an observation too.)

b. Add a little more yeast, then light a candle or splint and lower the flame into the jar above the liquid. What happens?

c. Blow out the candle and lower the glowing wick into the jar. What happens? What inferences can be made from your observations? (This is really an oxygen generator but students can only *infer* the presence of oxygen as they observe the burning candle flame up and burn faster and the glowing wick burst into flame again.)

Carbon Dioxide

For this activity you'll need:

—baking soda
—vinegar
—candle
—matches
—plastic shoebox (or some similar container)
—a peanut butter jar
—piece of clay

a. Pour about a cup of baking soda into the plastic shoebox.

b. Pour about 2 or 3 cups of vinegar onto the soda in the shoebox. What do you observe?

c. Lower a burning match into the shoebox just above the solution. What happens? Do it again. (Students should see that the flame goes out. They might *infer* that carbon dioxide has been generated and that explains why the flame goes out.)

d. Secure the candle with the clay to the bottom of the inside of the peanut butter jar. Then light the candle.

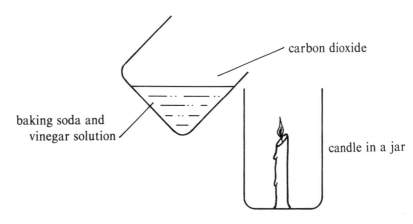

carbon dioxide

baking soda and
vinegar solution

candle in a jar

e. Add more baking soda and vinegar to the solution and quickly tip the shoebox as if to pour its contents over the candle, but do not let any of the solution come out. It takes a little practice pouring; do it again. What happens? (Students should observe that the candle is extinguished as the shoebox is tipped. They may *infer* that carbon dioxide was generated in the shoebox and put the flame out as it was poured over the candle.)

Resources

American Association for the Advancement of Science, *Science—A Process Approach: Commentary for Teachers,* Xerox Corporation, 1970.

American Geological Institute, *Investigating the Earth,* Houghton Mifflin Company, 1984.

B. C. Cartoons by permission of Johnny Hart and Field Enterprises Inc.

Butts, David P. and Gene E. Hall, *Children and Science: The Process of Teaching and Learning,* Prentice-Hall, Englewood Cliffs, New Jersey, 1975.

Drawings of the Newton Scale and Equal-Arm Balance were furnished by the Ohaus Scale Corporation.

Education Development Center, Elementary Science Study Unit *Attribute Games and Problems,* Webster Division, McGraw-Hill Book Company, 1968.

Education Development Center, Elementary Science Study Unit *Making Maps, Mapping and Mapping Games,* Webster Division, McGraw-Hill Book Company, 1971.

Education Development Center, Elementary Science Study Unit *Match and Measure,* Webster Division, McGraw-Hill Book Company, 1971.

Education Development Center, Elementary Science Study Unit *Peas and Particles,* Webster Division, McGraw-Hill Book Company, 1969.

Education Development Center, Elementary Science Study Unit *Pendulums,* Webster Division, McGraw-Hill Book Company, 1969.

Fisher, Merle, "Comedy with CO_2", *Science and Children* 20: 36–37, October, 1982.

Rabenau, Diane F., *The Metric System: Book 3,* Milliken Publishing Company, St. Louis, Missouri, 1974.

PART 2

The Integrated Science Process Skills

This part of the book deals with the integrated science process skills which are taught in the intermediate elementary grades. The preceding basic process skills provide a foundation for the more complex integrated science processes. All of the science process skills are necessary when one attempts to find solutions to scientific or other problems. The basic skills provide the intellectual groundwork in this problem-solving endeavor. On the other hand, the integrated skills serve as the immediate tools one uses when solving a problem. For example, the basic skill of observing is needed as observations (data) are collected when solving a problem. The interpretation of these observations (data) is a different skill—an integrated skill. Naturally a person must make good observations before he can interpret these observations. Thus, the basic process skills are prerequisite to the integrated skills. On the other hand, the integrated processes are the terminal skills one needs to *do* science experiments or to solve problems. These integrated skills consist of identifying variables, constructing tables of data and graphs, describing relationships between variables, acquiring and processing data, analyzing investigations, constructing hypotheses, operationally defining variables, designing investigations, and experimenting.

IDENTIFYING
VARIABLES 7

Purpose: In this chapter, you will be learning one of the skills needed when conducting an investigation. This important skill will be used throughout this section whenever you analyze how someone else conducted an investigation or whenever you plan and carry out an investigation of your own.

Objective: After studying this chapter you should be able to:

1. identify the manipulated and responding variables in a written statement or from a description of an investigation.

Approximate time for completion: 40 minutes

Note: Throughout the exercises in this section, you will be called upon to answer questions that require you to make measurements. It is assumed that you know how to measure mass, length, temperature, volume, and rate. If you are not sure that you know how to make these measurements, you may wish to review Chapter 4.

Use the spaces provided for recording your answers to the exercises.

The best way to become comfortable with science is to do science. You need to investigate a bit, use some equipment, and get your hands dirty. To accomplish this and also to learn how to identify variables, carry out the following activities.

Get the following items from the supply area:

4 baby food jars
thermometer
plastic spoon
large container (about a liter for holding water)
calcium chloride

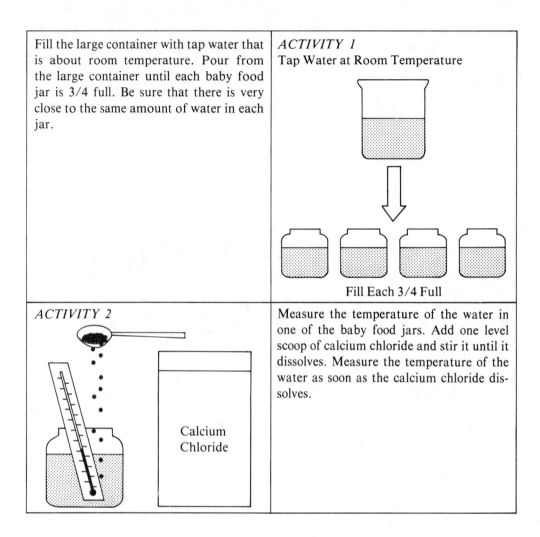

Fill the large container with tap water that is about room temperature. Pour from the large container until each baby food jar is 3/4 full. Be sure that there is very close to the same amount of water in each jar.	*ACTIVITY 1* Tap Water at Room Temperature Fill Each 3/4 Full
ACTIVITY 2 Calcium Chloride	Measure the temperature of the water in one of the baby food jars. Add one level scoop of calcium chloride and stir it until it dissolves. Measure the temperature of the water as soon as the calcium chloride dissolves.

1. Temperature of the water before _____ . After _____ .

2. What happened to the temperature of the water in the jar? _____

3. How many degrees did the temperature change when you added one level scoop of

   calcium chloride? _____

You probably found that the temperature increased about 3 to 5 degrees Celsius. The temperature could, of course, be more or less than this, depending on the amount of water you used and the amount of calcium chloride.

To keep track of your measurements, record them in Table 7-1. You should record both the number of spoons of calcium chloride added and the increase in temperature for the jar you completed (call it jar A).

Table 7-1

Jar	Number of Scoops of Calcium Chloride	Temperature Change (°C)
A B C D		

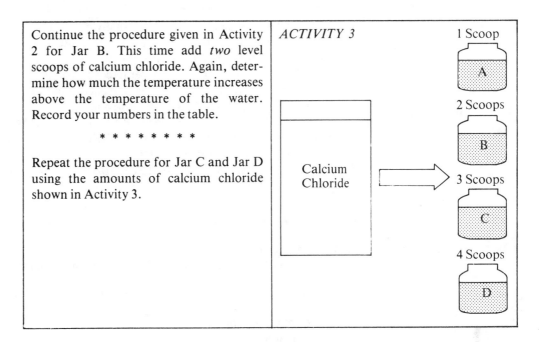

Continue the procedure given in Activity 2 for Jar B. This time add *two* level scoops of calcium chloride. Again, determine how much the temperature increases above the temperature of the water. Record your numbers in the table.

* * * * * * * *

Repeat the procedure for Jar C and Jar D using the amounts of calcium chloride shown in Activity 3.

ACTIVITY 3

Calcium Chloride

1 Scoop — A

2 Scoops — B

3 Scoops — C

4 Scoops — D

Your table of numbers should be complete now. It ought to look like the one that follows except for the last column. We recorded the numbers we got when we did the experiment. Your numbers will almost surely be different, depending on the amount of water in your jars and the size of scoop.

OUR NUMBERS ➤

Jar	Number of Scoops of Calcium Chloride	Temperature Change (°C)
A	1	5
B	2	9
C	3	14
D	4	21

Answer the following questions about what you did:

4. Did you use the same amount of water in each jar? _____

5. Did you use the same amount of calcium chloride in each jar? _____

6. Did the temperature change the same amount for each jar? _____

7. What prediction would you make if you added six scoops of calcium chloride to the

   same amount of water? _____

If you followed the directions carefully, you should have used the *same amount* of water in all four jars. You should have added *different amounts* of calcium chloride to each jar (1 scoop to Jar A, 2 to Jar B, 3 to Jar C and 4 to Jar D). The temperature should have *increased by different amounts* in the jars. The increase was greater for those jars in which more calcium chloride was dissolved. Finally, you probably predicted that the temperature change would be *even greater* if six scoops of calcium chloride were added.

In the last part of this chapter, you will complete a short unit of programmed instruction. Perhaps, you have never used this type of instruction before. If not, the procedure is very simple. The instruction is broken up into small pieces. These pieces are presented as frames. In a frame, some information is usually given; and a response is required of you, the learner. *After* writing in your response, you can check its accuracy by comparing it with the answer on the right hand side of the page.

Use a 3 × 5 card or a piece of paper to cover the answers. Read the frame and write in your response. Then slide the card down to check your answer. If you make a mistake, read the frame again to find out what went wrong.

THE PURPOSE OF THIS PROGRAM IS TO TEACH YOU TO IDENTIFY *VARIABLES*. AFTER YOU HAVE LEARNED TO IDENTIFY VARIABLES, YOU WILL LEARN TO CLASSIFY THEM AS *MANIPULATED* or *RESPONDING* VARIABLES. THESE WORDS ARE PROBABLY UNFAMILIAR TO YOU NOW, BUT SOON THEY WILL BE FAMILIAR.

Read this statement:

The height of bean plants depends on the amount of water they receive.

In the above statement, two variables are described:

1. height of bean plants
2. amount of water

A variable is something that can vary or change in a situation. What are the variables in this statement? The time it takes to run a kilometer depends on the amount of exercise a person gets. 8. _____ _____	<u>time to run a kilometer</u> <u>amount of exercise</u> It would not be correct to say just "time" or "exercise" as the variables because you must include how each variable will be measured. For example, "height of plant" would be a variable and "height" would not be a variable.
What are the variables in this statement? The higher the temperature of water, the faster an egg will cook. 9. _____ _____	<u>temperature of water</u> <u>time needed for an egg to cook</u> Your answers don't have to be exactly the same as these but they should be close.
An investigation was done to see if keeping the lights on for different amounts of time each day affected the number of eggs chickens layed. What are the variables in this investigation? 10. _____ _____	<u>hours (or amount) of light</u> <u>number of eggs</u> Again, your answers do not have to be exactly like this, but they should be similar. In particular, "light" or "eggs" would be incorrect listings for the variables.

What are the variables in this statement? Remember a variable is something that can change or vary in a situation. The temperature of the water was measured at different depths of a lake. 11. _____ _____	temperature of water distance below the surface Perhaps you said "Depth of lake" for the second variable.
Here is another statement. Identify the variables in it. Grass will grow taller if it is watered a great deal and is fertilized. 12. _____ _____	height of grass amount of water amount of fertilizer Many variables can be included in a statement. You may find one, two, three, or more.
Think back to the investigation you did at the beginning of this chapter. Then complete this statement: If the amount of calcium chloride added to the water increases, the temperature of the water 13. _____ (increases, decreases)	increases Clearly, the more scoops of calcium chloride, the more the water temperature increased.
What were the variables in the investigation you carried out? (HINT: look back at the statement in Frame 13) 14. _____ _____	number of scoops of calcium chloride temperature change of water You might have said "amount of calcium chloride" or "temperature of water." These answers would be correct also.
If a variable is deliberately changed in a situation, it is called a manipulated variable. Which of the two variables was the manipulated variable in your investigation? 15. _____ _____	*number of scoops of calcium chloride* You deliberately used a different number of scoops for each jar so you *manipulated* this variable.

What variable is being manipulated in this investigation? The amount of pollution produced by cars was measured for cars using gasoline containing different amounts of lead. 16. _____	amount of lead in gasoline
What is the manipulated variable in this situation? Lemon trees receiving the most water produce the largest lemons. 17. _____	amount of water The "amount of water" could be manipulated or changed to determine its effect on the size of the lemons produced.
Identify the manipulated variable in this situation: The amount of algae growth in lakes seems to be directly related to the number of sacks of phosphate fertilizer sold by the local merchants. 18. _____	number of sacks of phosphate fertilizer sold
An investigation was performed to see if corn seeds would sprout at different times depending on the temperature of the water in which they were placed. What is the manipulated variable? 19. _____	temperature of water In each of the last four frames, one variable was changed to see what would happen. A variable that is deliberately changed is called a manipulated variable.

The more water you put on grass, the taller it will grow.

"Amount of water" is the manipulated variable in the above statement. The other variable is the "height of grass." It is called the *RESPONDING VARIABLE.* The variable that may change as a *result* of the manipulation is called the responding variable.

(GO ON TO THE NEXT FRAME)

Identify the manipulated and responding variables in this statement: More bushels of potatoes will be produced if the soil is fertilized more. 20. Manipulated variable: _____ Responding variable: _____	<u>amount of fertilizer</u> (manipulated variable) <u>number of bushels of potatoes</u> (responding variable) The amount of fertilizer could be *manipulated* to see if the number of bushels of potatoes *responded*.
Think back to the investigation you did at the beginning of this chapter. You manipulated the amount of calcium chloride. What was the responding variable? 21. _____	<u>temperature change of water</u> In each container, you *manipulated* the amount of calcium chloride to see if the temperature of the water would *respond*.
Look at the sketch to the right. It shows an investigation similar to the one you did. Notice that *different* amounts of water are used in each jar, with one scoop of calcium chloride added to each jar. After the calcium chloride dissolves, the temperature change in each jar will be determined.	PUT *ONE* SCOOP IN *EACH* JAR
What are the manipulated (MV) and responding (RV) variables in this investigation? 22. MV _____ RV _____	(MV) <u>amount of water</u> (RV) <u>temperature change of water</u> This is similar to the investigation you did, but now a different variable is being manipulated.

What are the manipulated and responding variables in this investigation?	(MV) <u>amount of Vitamin A</u> (RV) <u>weight of rats</u>
Five groups of rats are fed identical diets except for the amount of Vitamin A that they receive. Each group gets a different amount. After three weeks on the diet, the rats are weighed to see if the amount of Vitamin A received has affected their weight. 23. MV _____ RV _____	If the "amount of Vitamin A" is manipulated or changed, then perhaps the "weight of rats" will respond. Of course, weight may not be affected if Vitamin A is not essential. The "weight of rats" is still the responding variable whether or not it is actually affected by the manipulated variable.
An experiment was done with six groups of children to see if scores on their weekly spelling tests were affected by the number of minutes of spelling practice they had each day. 24. MV _____ RV _____	(MV) <u>minutes of spelling practice</u> (RV) <u>score on spelling test</u>
PROBLEM: Will the number of nails picked up by an electromagnet be increased if more batteries are put in the circuit? Suppose an investigation was carried out on the problem above. What would the variables be? 25. MV _____ RV _____	(MV) <u>number of batteries in circuit</u> (RV) <u>number of nails picked up</u>

In this chapter, you have learned to identify variables. You learned that a *variable* is something that can change or vary. Next, you learned to identify two different kinds of variables. A variable that is deliberately changed in a situation is called a *manipulated* variable. The variable that may change as a result of the manipulation is called the *responding* variable.

Now take the self-test for Chapter 7 and check your answers.

Continue into Chapter 8 or return to Chapter 7 for more study as you see fit, based on the results of your self-test.

Self-test for Chapter 7:

IDENTIFYING VARIABLES

For each of the following statements or descriptions identify the manipulated variable (MV) and responding variable (RV). The answers will follow.

1. Students in a science class carried out an investigation in which a flashlight was pointed at a screen. They wished to find out if the distance from the light to the screen had any effect on the size of the illuminated area.

   MV _____

   RV _____

2. The number of pigs in a litter is determined by the weight of the mother pig.

   MV _____

   RV _____

3. *PROBLEM:* The State Agriculture Department has been counting the number of foxes in Brown County. Will the number of foxes have any effect on the rabbit population?

   MV _____

   RV _____

4. The score on the final test depends on the number of subordinate skills attained.

   MV _____

   RV _____

5. *INVESTIGATION:* A study was done with white rats to see if the number of offspring born dead was affected by the number of minutes of exposure to X-rays by the mother rats.

   MV _____

   RV _____

SELF-TEST ANSWERS: Identifying Variables

1. MV distance from light to screen
   RV size of illuminated area
2. MV weight of mother pig
   RV number of pigs in litter
3. MV number of foxes
   RV number of rabbits
4. MV number of subordinate skills attained
   RV score on final test
5. MV minutes of exposure to X-rays
   RV number of offspring born dead

CONSTRUCTING A TABLE OF DATA 8

Purpose: There are a number of skills that are useful when conducting an investigation. One of these is the organization of measurements (data) into tables. The purpose of a data table is to organize a great deal of information in an efficient manner.

Objectives: After studying the information in this chapter you should be able to:

1. construct a table of data when given a graph.
2. construct a table of data when given a written description of the measurements made during an investigation.

Approximate time for completion: 35 minutes

Place a sheet of paper over this page. Slide the paper down just ahead of the area you are reading. The appearance of three "X's" across the center of the page such as:

X　　　　　　　　X　　　　　　　　X

will signal that the correct responses to the question asked will appear next.

Reading a graph is similar to reading a map. One difference is that both edges of the graph are labeled with numbers instead of letters as are most maps.

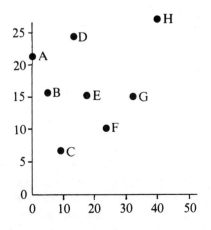

A point on a graph is described using the values given on the horizontal and vertical axes. Imagine a vertical line drawn through the point labeled "E" on the graph on page 95. Such a line would intersect the horizontal axis at the point with a value of 18. Imagine a second line drawn horizontally through point E. This line would intersect the vertical axis at the point with a value of 15. Therefore, point E would be described as (18, 15).

Follow this rule when describing the location of a point on a graph:

Always write the value from the horizontal axis (bottom line) first. Separate the two numbers with a comma and enclose them in parentheses.

Write the pair of numbers that describe point "H" on the graph on page 95.

1. _____

       X   X   X

(40, 27)

Now write the number pair that describe each of these points on the graph on page 95.

2. A _____   5. D _____
3. B _____   6. F _____
4. C _____   7. G _____

      X   X   X

(0, 21)   (13, 24)
(5, 16)   (25, 10)
(10, 6)   (31, 15)

Your answers may be slightly different from those above but there should not be great differences. For example (14, 22) would not be wrong for 5.

When an investigation is carried out, the measurements made are called data. Measurements of time, temperature, and volume are examples of data. The measurements of data are usually written in a data table.

When recording a table of data, the measurements of the *manipulated variable* are usually ordered. To order data means that the numbers are arranged from smallest to largest *or* from largest to smallest, which ever the data gatherer desires. Most of the time it is desirable to order from smallest to largest.

The SAME FIVE NUMBER PAIRS (5, 7) (3, 3) (9, 5) (1, 6) (2, 4) were used in each of the following tables of data. The first number in the pair is the manipulated variable and the second number refers to the responding variable. Which tables have been correctly ordered?

8.

A. MV	RV	B. MV	RV	C. MV	RV	D. MV	RV	E. MV	RV
5	7	3	3	1	3	1	6	9	5
3	3	2	4	2	4	2	4	5	7
9	5	9	5	3	5	3	3	3	3
1	6	1	6	5	6	5	7	2	4
2	4	5	7	9	7	9	5	1	6

      X   X   X

D and *E* are correct. *A* has none of the data ordered. In *B* the responding variable data has been ordered. This should not occur unless it just happens when the manipulated variable data is ordered. To achieve *C* it was necessary to separate the number pairs. This should not be done. *E* is a correct answer. It is just not the most common method.

Try ordering the following number pairs in the table. Assume the first number in each pair is for the manipulated variable.

9. (20, 17)   (5, 18)   (9, 12)   (23, 26)   (17, 3)

MV	RV

X   X   X

Either is correct

MV	RV
5	18
9	12
17	3
20	17
23	26

MV	RV
23	26
20	17
17	3
9	12
5	18

10. Try one more. Remember (MV, RV): (1, 12) (12, 12) (13, 10) (5, 10) (8, 12)

MV	RV

X   X   X

MV	RV
1	12
5	10
8	12
12	12
13	10

MV	RV
13	10
12	12
8	12
5	10
1	12

11. Here is a written description of an account of an investigation. Notice that some of the data have already been recorded in a table. Now read the paragraph and order the next four pairs of numbers.

The heights that balls bounced when dropped different distances were measured. A ball dropped 50 cm bounced 40 cm high. A 10 cm drop bounced 8 cm. A ball bounced 24 cm when dropped 30 cm. The bounce was 56 cm high for a 70 cm drop. A 100 cm drop bounced 80 cm.

Length of drop (cm)	Height of bounce (cm)
10	8

X   X   X

Length of drop (cm)	Height of bounce (cm)
10	8
30	24
50	40
70	56
100	80

The columns could have been reversed. There is no rule that states which side of a table should contain the manipulated variable. Usually the manipulated variable is written on the left but not always.

12. Here is another problem to practice on. Record these data in the table provided.

   The distance covered by a runner during each second of a race was measured. During the 15th second of the race the runner covered two meters. Three meters were covered during the 12th second. Four meters were covered during the 9th second. During the 6th second three meters were covered. During the 3rd second, two meters were traveled.

Time during race (sec)	Distance covered (meters)

X   X   X

Time during race (sec)	Distance covered (meters)
3	2
6	3
9	4
12	3
15	2

13. Now try something a little different. Construct an ordered table of data showing points on a graph. Complete the following table of data by studying the accompanying graph. The first two points on the graph have already been recorded.

Amount of rain (cm)	Weight of fruit (kg)
45	125
55	140

X   X   X

Amount of rain (cm)	Weight of fruit (kg)
45	125
55	140
60	150
66	200
70	280
75	310
80	350
90	350

The answers don't have to be the same as these but they should be close.

14. Complete the ordered table of data given below. The first two points on the graph have already been recorded.

Heating time (min)	Temperature of water (C)
1	45
2	50

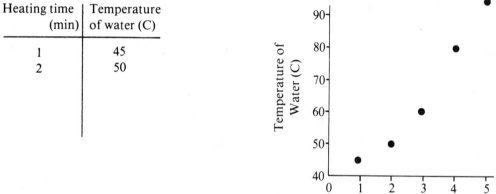

X   X   X

Heating time (min)	Temperature of water (C)
1	45
2	50
3	60
4	80
5	95

15. Now construct a table of data for the graph given below. First label the columns with the proper headings. Copy these from the horizontal and vertical axes of the graph. Don't forget to include the units in which the variables were measured.

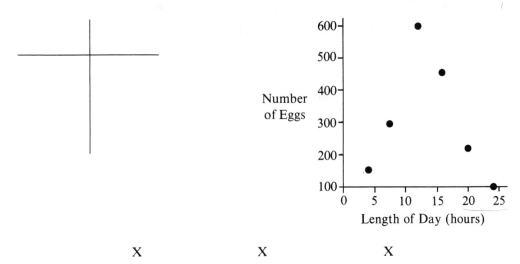

X   X   X

Length of day (hours)	Number of eggs
4	150
8	300
12	600
16	450
20	225
24	100

There are two reasons why it is important to do the kind of tasks in this chapter. First, you will need the skills in order to organize data for any investigation you will perform. In later chapters you will be given the opportunity to perform investigations and it may be necessary to produce tables of data. Secondly, the skill of organizing a data table is helpful in learning to do just the opposite. In the next chapter you will learn to make a graph from a data table and the experience gained in this chapter will be helpful.

Now take the self-test for Chapter 8.

Self-test for Constructing a Table of Data

1. Construct a table of data from this graph.

Height of Corn (cm) vs Hours of Sunlight

2. Construct an ordered table of data for the following.

The length of shadows made by sticks of different length were measured. A stick 50 cm long made a shadow 40 cm long. The shadow was 5 cm long for a stick 10 cm. A 30 cm stick made a shadow 22 cm long and a stick 40 cm long made a shadow of 29 cm. The shadow was 12 cm for a stick 20 cm long.

Length of stick (cm)	Length of shadow (cm)

3. Write the number pair that describes the location of each point.

A _____

B _____

C _____

D _____

E _____

F _____

SELF-TEST ANSWERS:

Constructing a Table of Data

1.

Hours of sunlight	Height of corn (cm)
20	1
40	1
60	2
80	6
100	10

2.

Length of stick (cm)	Length of shadow (cm)
10	5
20	12
30	22
40	29
50	40

3. A. (5, 42)
   B. (3, 26)
   C. (15, 10)
   D. (17, 45)
   E. (20, 25)
   F. (30, 50)

CONSTRUCTING A GRAPH 9

Purpose: "A picture is worth a thousand words." Almost everyone has heard this famous saying. Often it is true that information can be communicated more easily with a picture instead of using a spoken or written message. Your task in this chapter is to learn to draw one special kind of picture—a graph.

Objective: After studying this chapter you should be able to:

1. construct a graph when provided with a brief description of an investigation and a table of data.

Approximate time for completion: 45 minutes

An example of what you will be able to do when you finish this chapter is shown below. You will be given the type of information found on the left hand side of the page and will be expected to produce the type of material found on the right hand side.

You will be given:

INVESTIGATION: Beans were soaked in water for different lengths of time and their gain in mass was recorded.

Soaking time (min)	Gain in mass (g)
5	10
10	20
15	40
20	45
25	50

You will produce:

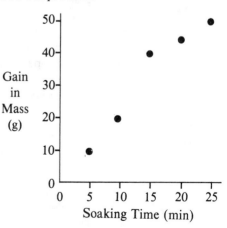

That part of the above graph labeled "gain in mass" is called the vertical *axis* and that part labeled "soaking time" is called the horizontal *axis*. Together they make up the *axes* of the graph.

Amount of fertilizer (kg)	Height of plants (cm)
2	24
4	50
6	74
8	38
10	20

Suppose you wished to construct a graph of the table of data given above. What would you have to do? After drawing the horizontal and vertical axes, the variables from the data table are written along these axes. When deciding which variable to assign to which axis follow this rule:

The manipulated variable is always written along the horizontal axis. The responding variable is always written along the vertical axis.

In the case shown above, the amount of fertilizer was deliberately manipulated and the height of the plants was then measured. So, "amount of fertilizer (kg)" should be written along the horizontal axis and "height of plants (cm)" should be written beside the vertical axis. The correct form is shown on the graph below:

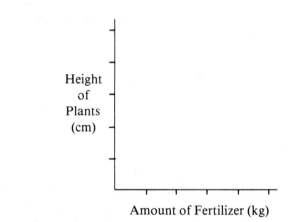

Height of Plants (cm)

Amount of Fertilizer (kg)

Following are the descriptions of several investigations. Beside each description is a graph with the variable assigned to the axes. Your task is to determine whether the assignment is proper.

1. *INVESTIGATION:* A ball is dropped from several *distances above* the *floor* and the *height* it *bounces* up is then measured.

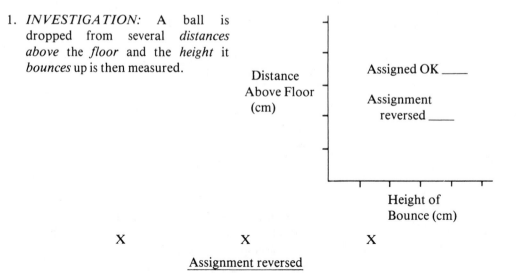

Distance Above Floor (cm)

Assigned OK ____

Assignment reversed ____

Height of Bounce (cm)

X   X   X

Assignment reversed

Since the ball was deliberately dropped from a certain height, that variable is manipulated and should be assigned to the horizontal axis.

2. *INVESTIGATION:* A candle was burned under glass jars of different volumes to see if the length of *time the candle burns* is affected by the *volume* of the *jar.*

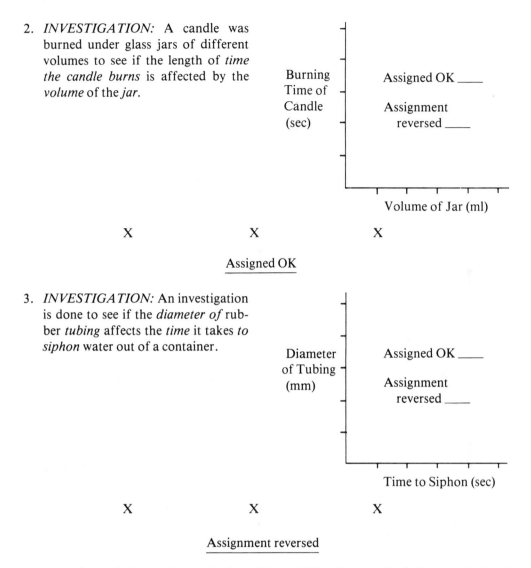

Burning Time of Candle (sec)

Assigned OK _____

Assignment reversed _____

Volume of Jar (ml)

X   X   X

Assigned OK

3. *INVESTIGATION:* An investigation is done to see if the *diameter of* rubber *tubing* affects the *time* it takes *to siphon* water out of a container.

Diameter of Tubing (mm)

Assigned OK _____

Assignment reversed _____

Time to Siphon (sec)

X   X   X

Assignment reversed

Several descriptions of investigations follow. Write the variable being manipulated along the horizontal axis for each graph. Write the variable expected to respond along the vertical axis. Don't forget to indicate in what units each variable is to be measured.

4. *INVESTIGATION:* A fisherman used several different sized hooks and recorded the number of fish caught on each.

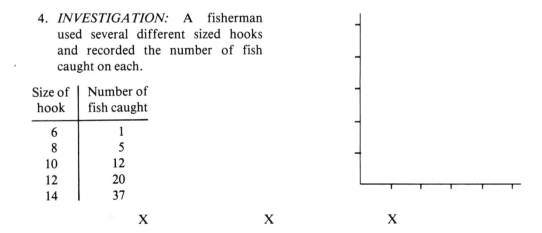

Size of hook	Number of fish caught
6	1
8	5
10	12
12	20
14	37

X   X   X

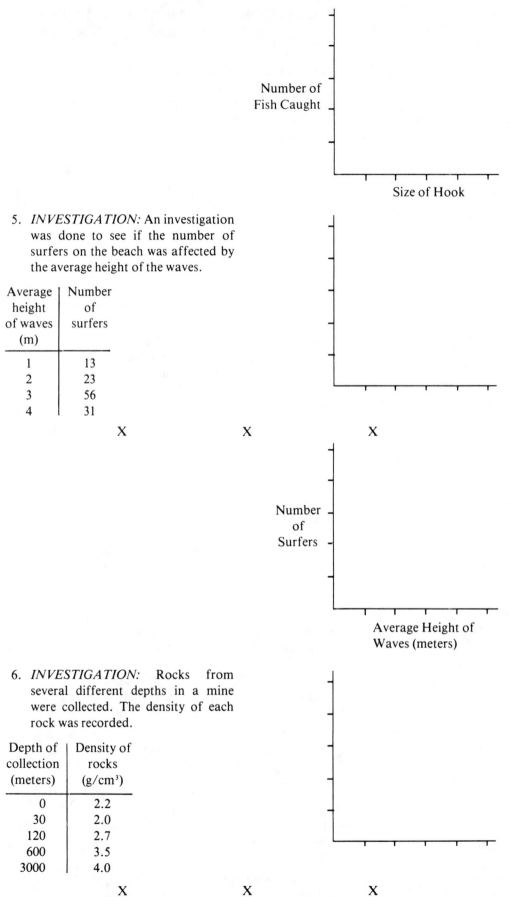

Number of Fish Caught

Size of Hook

5. *INVESTIGATION:* An investigation was done to see if the number of surfers on the beach was affected by the average height of the waves.

Average height of waves (m)	Number of surfers
1	13
2	23
3	56
4	31

X   X   X

Number of Surfers

Average Height of Waves (meters)

6. *INVESTIGATION:* Rocks from several different depths in a mine were collected. The density of each rock was recorded.

Depth of collection (meters)	Density of rocks (g/cm³)
0	2.2
30	2.0
120	2.7
600	3.5
3000	4.0

X   X   X

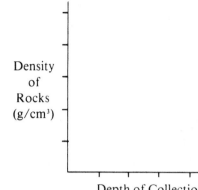

Remember this: the manipulated variable is usually written in the left column of a data table, but not always. Read the description of an investigation before deciding which variable has been manipulated.

In order to construct a graph from a table of data, you must learn to do three things. You just learned to do one of them when you practiced writing the variables along the proper axes. The second thing you need to learn to do is place a number scale on each axis.

To label an axis with a numerical scale remember the following steps. Each of the steps is illustrated with a sample problem. For example, if the values to be graphed were those shown below:

7
12
22
48
55

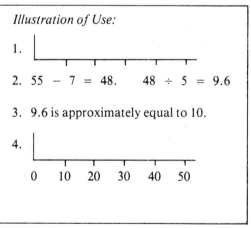

Proper Steps:
1. Mark off the axis into about five equal line segments.
2. Subtract the smallest value of the variable from the largest and divide by 5.
3. Round the answer to the nearest commonly used counting number (e.g., 2, 3, 4, 5, 10, 15, etc.)
4. Begin with a number equal to or slightly less than the smallest number to be graphed and label the axis with the selected interval.

Illustration of Use:
1.
2. $55 - 7 = 48$. $48 \div 5 = 9.6$
3. 9.6 is approximately equal to 10.
4.
   0   10   20   30   40   50

A table of data is given below. Three axes for each variable are shown also. For each of the axes determine if it is properly labeled. If you think the graph is *not* done properly, check the reason for it being wrong. For questions 7-12, refer to the following table:

Average cost of watch ($)	Error per month (minutes)
249	2
225	4
220	5
200	6
124	9
110	10

7.

```
  |
  |_____
  0   50  100  150  200  250
     Average Cost of Watch ($)
```

A. Label OK ____

B. Difference between numbers not equal ____

C. Too many numbers ____

D. Too few numbers ____

E. Start with too small number ____

X   X   X

E, by starting with 0 only about half of the available space on the graph is used. The first number on the label should be the smallest number to be graphed or some number only slightly smaller. By no means is it necessary to start with 0. For instance, in the above problem the first number should have been 110 or some number just smaller than 110.

8.

```
  |
  |_____
  110  124  200  220  225  249
       Average Cost of Watch ($)
```

A. Label OK ____

B. Difference between numbers not equal ____

C. Too many numbers ____

D. Too few numbers ____

E. Start with too small number ____

X   X   X

B, the difference between 110 and 124 is not the same as the difference between 124 and 200. The intervals should be equal.

9.

```
  |
  |_____
  100  130  160  190  220  250
       Average Cost of Watch ($)
```

A. Label OK ____

B. Difference between numbers not equal ____

C. Too many numbers ____

D. Too few numbers ____

E. Start with too small number ____

X   X   X

A, graph is correctly labeled.

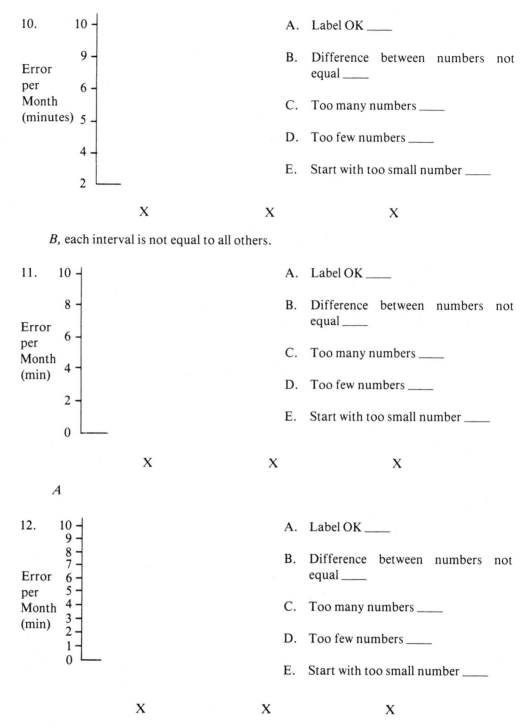

10.   10 ┤

        9 ┤

Error
per   6 ┤
Month
(minutes) 5 ┤

        4 ┤

        2 └──┴──

        A. Label OK ____

        B. Difference between numbers not equal ____

        C. Too many numbers ____

        D. Too few numbers ____

        E. Start with too small number ____

            X   X   X

B, each interval is not equal to all others.

11.   10 ┤

        8 ┤

Error   6 ┤
per
Month   4 ┤
(min)
        2 ┤

        0 └──┴──

        A. Label OK ____

        B. Difference between numbers not equal ____

        C. Too many numbers ____

        D. Too few numbers ____

        E. Start with too small number ____

            X   X   X

    A

12.   10 ┤
        9 ┤
        8 ┤
        7 ┤
Error   6 ┤
per   5 ┤
Month   4 ┤
(min)   3 ┤
        2 ┤
        1 ┤
        0 └──┴──

        A. Label OK ____

        B. Difference between numbers not equal ____

        C. Too many numbers ____

        D. Too few numbers ____

        E. Start with too small number ____

            X   X   X

C, there are too many numbers cluttering the scale; 5 or 6 would be better than the 10 numbers shown.

You have just had some practice in distinguishing between proper and improper numerical scales. In the next exercise you will use your skills and make some scales of your own.

Mark off the horizontal axis of the following graph outline into five equal line segments. Use a series of small marks across the axis. Mark off the vertical axis into five equal line segments also.

13.

Height of plant (cm)	Number of leaves
36	68
42	73
47	90
53	116
57	216

Number
of
Leaves

Height of Plant (cm)

Now you must place a number beside each mark on the graph. Examine the table of data above. What is the difference between the largest and the smallest value for the manipulated variable? Divide that number by 5. The difference between 36 and 57 is 21. When 21 is divided by 5 the result is 4.2. Rounding to the nearest commonly used counting number gives 4. Most people find 4 an easy number to count by. The smallest number you must graph is 36. This would make a good number to start numbering with.

14. Label each mark on the horizontal axis of 13 in jumps or intervals of 4. Begin at the corner of the graph with the number 36.

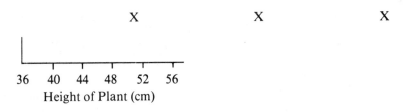

36   40   44   48   52   56
Height of Plant (cm)

Look back at the data table in 13 again. What is the difference between the largest and the smallest value for the responding variable? Divide that number by 5. Most people can count by 30's easier than by 29's. So round your counting number off to 30. Starting with 68 would make counting difficult. It would be better to drop down to some smaller number like 60.

15. Starting with 60, label the vertical axis of 13 in jumps of 30. Begin at the corner of the graph.

X   X   X

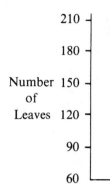

Here is a second problem to work on. Label the axes with proper numerical scales for graphing the data in the table below. Remember to mark off each axis with about 5 marks and then devise an appropriate numerical scale for each.

16.

Time from start of hatching (hours)	Number of flies hatched
9	25
12	153
14	269
15	617
18	1245

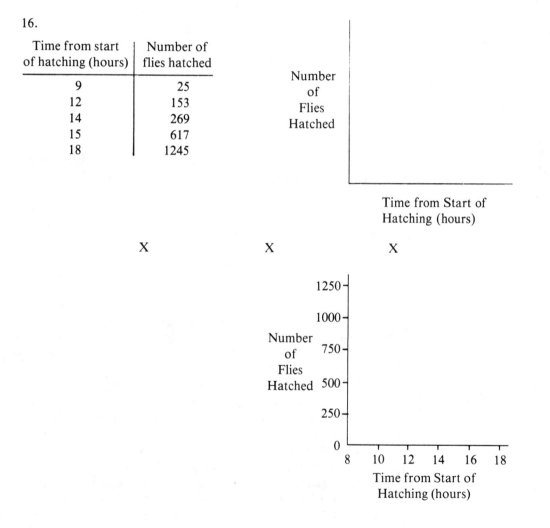

17. Here is the last problem on making a number scale. Label the axes with proper numerical scales for graphing these data.

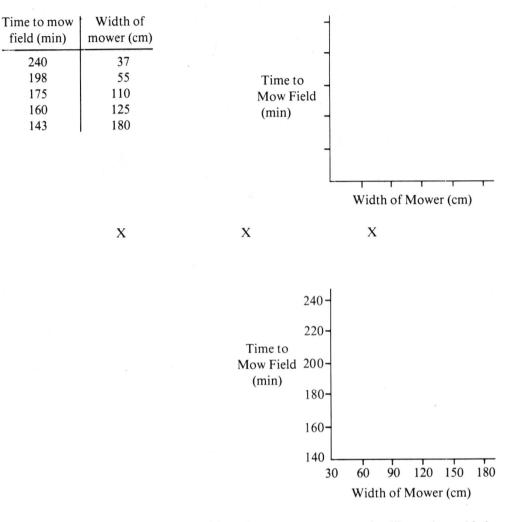

Time to mow field (min)	Width of mower (cm)
240	37
198	55
175	110
160	125
143	180

Time to Mow Field (min)

Width of Mower (cm)

X   X   X

Time to Mow Field (min)

240 –
220 –
200 –
180 –
160 –
140 ⌐

30   60   90   120   150   180

Width of Mower (cm)

The third and final skill you need in order to construct a graph will now be tackled. When you have axes drawn, variables written along the proper axes, and number scales made, you are ready to locate the position of the points on the graph.

18. Following is presented a table of data collected from an investigation. Also shown are the labeled axes to be used. What you have to do is mark the location of the number pairs. The first pair of numbers in the data table is 8 and 6. Locate 8 on the horizontal axis and 6 on the vertical axis . . . straight up from 8 and straight across from 6. Where these imaginary lines cross is a tiny • . Look at the second pair of numbers in the table. It will be located at the point (10, 15) on the graph. Sight straight up from 10 and straight across from 15. Where these imaginary two lines cross, a second small • is located. Now you locate the positions of the other three number pairs from the table in the same way. Mark the location of each with a small • on the graph.

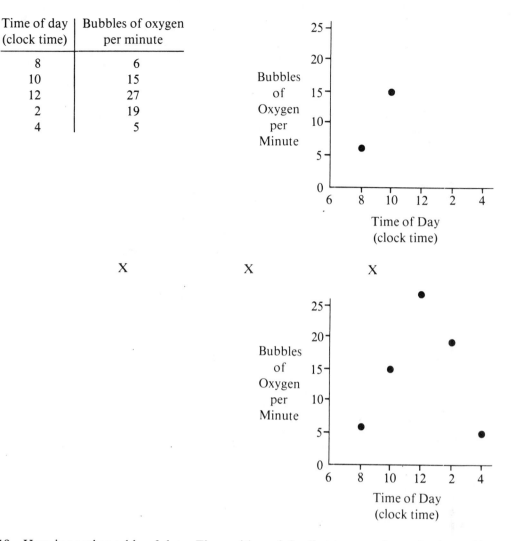

Time of day (clock time)	Bubbles of oxygen per minute
8	6
10	15
12	27
2	19
4	5

X   X   X

19. Here is another table of data. The position of the first two number pairs from this table are already located on the graph. You locate the other three points.

Temperature of freezer (°C)	Time to freeze (min)
−27	14
−20	20
−13	30
− 8	43
0	65

X   X   X

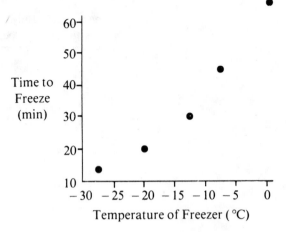

20.   Locate the position of the number pairs on the graph from this table of data.

Distance from bulb (cm)	Temperature of air (°C)
5	55
10	40
15	31
20	28
25	25

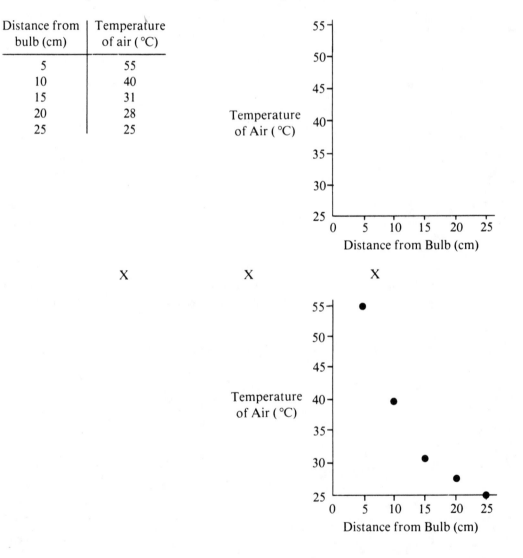

X   X   X

21. Locate the positions of the number pairs in this table on the graph.

Date in November	No. of books checked out
8	675
13	353
15	430
17	515
20	270

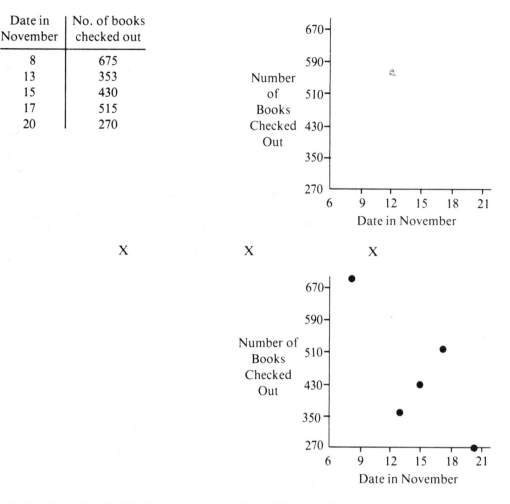

X   X   X

You have just finished practice on the third skill you will need in order to construct a graph. All you have to do now is put together the skills you have just learned and you will be able to construct a graph.

Remember, for a graph to be properly constructed three things must be done:

a. The variables are written along the proper axes (of course, you may have to draw the axes first).
b. Each axis is labeled with an appropriate numerical scale.
c. The location of each pair of numbers is indicated.

In the last part of this chapter you will examine several graphs to see if they have been properly drawn. Then you will be given a description of an investigation and a table of data and will be expected to draw a graph.

An investigation and table of data follow. Two graphs of the data are shown also. For each of the graphs determine whether it is properly drawn. If you think the graph is not done properly, check what is wrong.

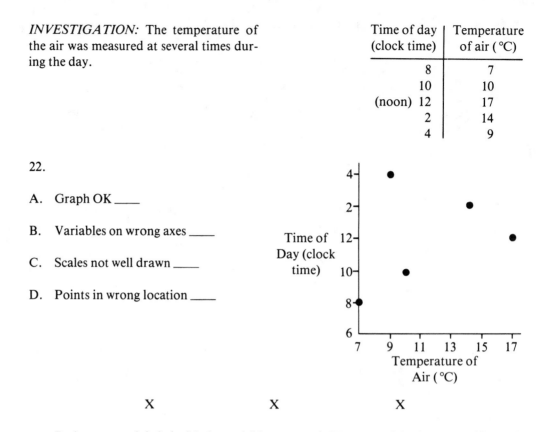

INVESTIGATION: The temperature of the air was measured at several times during the day.

Time of day (clock time)	Temperature of air (°C)
8	7
10	10
(noon) 12	17
2	14
4	9

22.

A.   Graph OK ____

B.   Variables on wrong axes ____

C.   Scales not well drawn ____

D.   Points in wrong location ____

X   X   X

B, the axes are labeled with the variables reversed. The *time of day* is the manipulated variable so it should be on the horizontal axes.

23.

A.   Graph OK ____

B.   Variables on wrong axes ____

C.   Scales not well drawn ____

D.   Points in wrong location ____

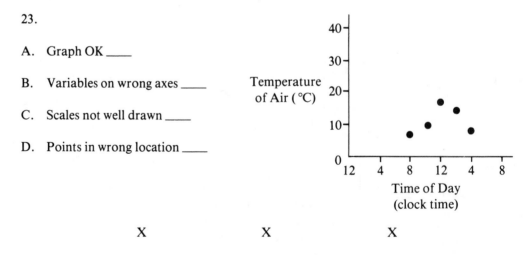

X   X   X

C, the numerical scales on both axes are too large. Notice that the points are all in a small lump. With appropriate scales the points should be distributed across the graph.
Now try putting all three skills together.

24. Construct a graph of data in this table.

INVESTIGATION: The number of kilometers per liter of gasoline was measured for cars traveling at different speeds.

Speed of car (km/h)	Kilometers per liter
20	6
25	5
30	4
40	3
50	2

X   X   X

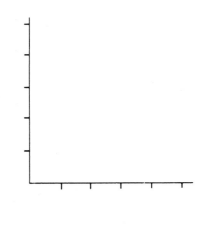

Try one more problem. Construct a graph for the data from this investigation.

25. *INVESTIGATION:* The average weight of ten pumpkins growing in a patch was determined at different times after planting.

Time after planting (weeks)	Average weight of pumpkins (kg)
2	0
7	0
9	1
12	9
18	22

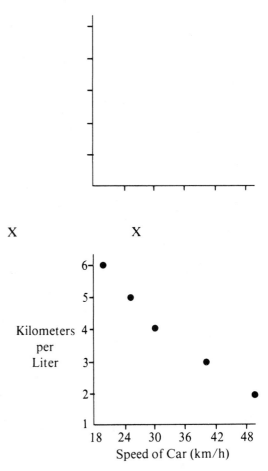

X   X   X

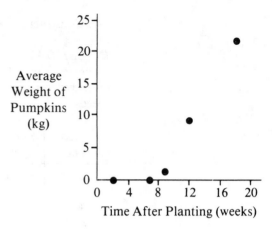

This is the last one.

26. *INVESTIGATION:* A box was dropped from an airplane and the distance it had fallen was measured after various lengths of time.

Time (sec)	Distance fallen (m)
1	5
2	20
3	45
4	80
5	125

X   X   X

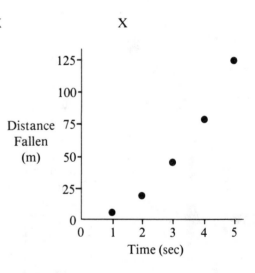

Let's see where you stand now. You have just learned to construct a graph of the data in a table. This is a valuable skill you will use later in this program and, hopefully, in many other places. In Chapter 10 you will learn how to make a written description of a graph.

Now take the self-test for Chapter 9.

Self-test for Constructing a Graph

1. Construct a graph of the data in this table.

   INVESTIGATION: Ice cubes of different sizes are melted in a pan of water.

Mass of ice cubes (grams)	Time to melt (minutes)
35	2
45	3
52	5
61	9
70	11

2. Locate the position of the number pairs from this investigation on the graph.

   INVESTIGATION: The number of letters that could be correctly identified on an eye chart at different distances was investigated.

Distance of eye from chart (m)	No. of letters identified
1	18
2	22
3	35
4	30
5	26

   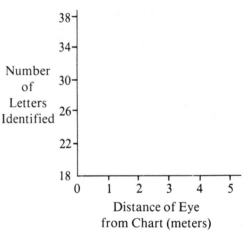

3. Label the axes with proper numerical scales for graphing these data. DO *NOT* locate the points.

   INVESTIGATION: The temperature of the air was measured on different days to see if it affected the number of swimmers on the beach.

Temperature of air (°C)	Number of swimmers
12	30
19	80
20	225
26	450
31	475

   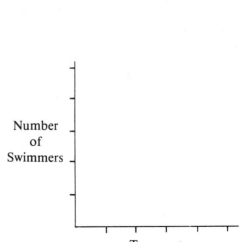

4. a. Write the variables from this investigation along the proper axes of the graph.

   INVESTIGATION: The *temperature of the water* was varied in several containers to see if the *time to evaporate* the water was affected.

   b. What is the rule used to assign variables to the axes of a graph?

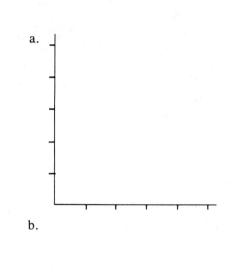

a.

b.

SELF-TEST ANSWERS: Constructing a Graph

1.

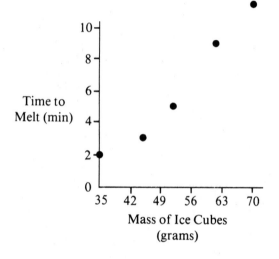

Note: To be correct
   a. the variables must be written along the axes as shown here
   b. the number scales should be about the same as this—if you numbered from 0 to 70 by 10's on the horizontal scale, it is wrong.

2.

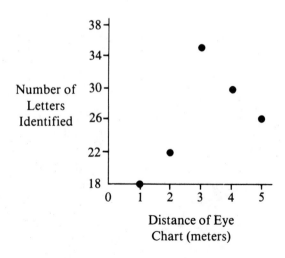

3.

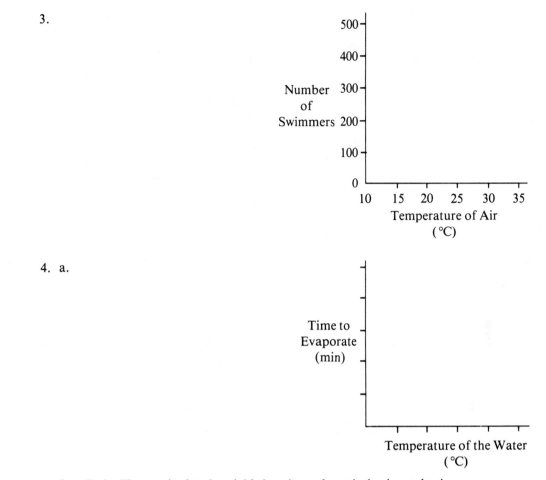

4. a.

b.   **Rule:** The manipulated variable is written along the horizontal axis.

DESCRIBING RELATIONSHIPS BETWEEN VARIABLES 10

Purpose: In the last two chapters you have learned to organize data in a table and to construct a graph. One other skill associated with graphing needs to be learned—the skill of interpreting a graph.

    You might think of a graph as a coded message; it means a great deal to the person who understands the code but not much to anyone else.

Objectives: After studying the information in this chapter you should be able to:

1. when given a graph, draw a best-fit line.
2. describe in writing the relationship between variables on a graph.

Approximate time for completion: 45 minutes

    First you will learn to draw a line of best-fit. The rules for constructing a best-fit line for a set of points on a graph are:

1. The line should be a straight line or a smooth curve.
2. All points should either lie on the line or very near to it.
3. There should be approximately equal number of points on either side of the line.

For example, examine the lines drawn on the graphs shown below. They are examples of best-fit lines.

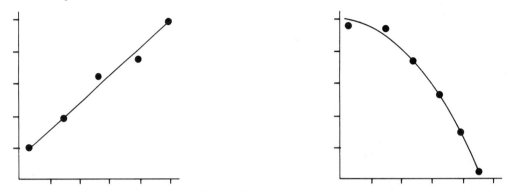

Notice that in both cases the best-fit line either passes directly through or very near all the points. If the points do not lie directly on the line, there are approximately equal numbers of points on either side of the best-fit line.

Shown below are several graphs with lines drawn through the data points. You are to decide whether it is a best-fit line. If you decide the line is not the "best-fit" check the reason.

1. A. Line is best-fit _____

    B. Should be curved _____

    C. Should be straight _____

    D. Too many data points on one side _____

    E. Curve not smooth _____

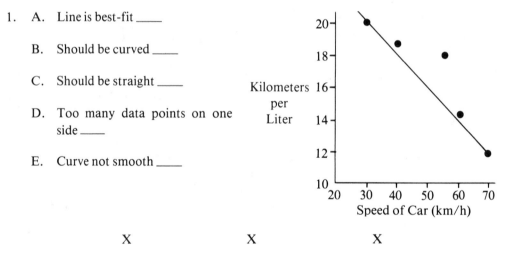

X   X   X

D, the line should be moved a little toward the upper right. You may have checked *B* also. A curved line could be used here.

2. A. Line is best-fit _____

    B. Should be curved _____

    C. Should be straight _____

    D. Too many data points on one side _____

    E. Curve not smooth _____

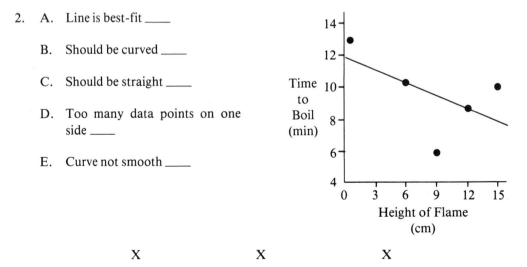

X   X   X

B, some of the points are a long way from the straight line. A curved line drawn in the shape of a "U" would fit better.

3. A. Line is best-fit ____

    B. Should be curved ____

    C. Should be straight ____

    D. Too many data points on one side ____

    E. Curve not smooth ____

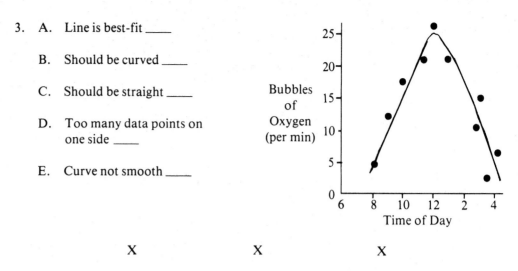

X   X   X

A, notice that the line seems to "average" the points. Some are above the line and some are below.

4. A. Line is best-fit ____

    B. Should be curved ____

    C. Should be straight ____

    D. Too many data points on one side ____

    E. Curve not smooth ____

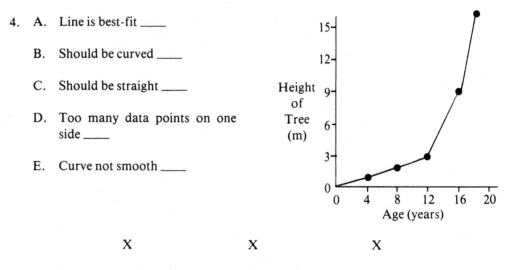

X   X   X

E, a best-fit line never jumps from point to point in straight line segments. If it curves it should be a *smooth* curve. For the graph above a smooth curve shaped like a "J" would probably be the line of best-fit.

5. A. Line is best-fit ____

    B. Should be curved ____

    C. Should be straight ____

    D. Too many data points on one side ____

    E. Curve not smooth ____

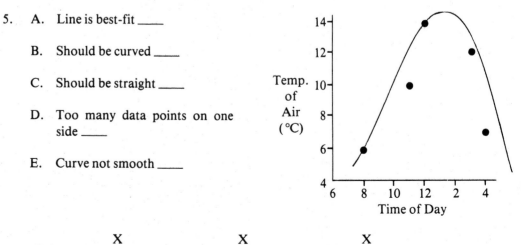

X   X   X

D, there are more points on the inside of the curve than on the outside. The curved line should probably be lowered a little in order to average the points on the graph.

Now try a little practice drawing best-fit lines for the graphs below. First decide whether a straight or curved line fits the points best. Then draw in the line. Try to make your lines "average out" the points on the graph. A good line of best-fit will usually pass through a few points, be above some others and below still others.

6. Draw best-fit lines for these points.

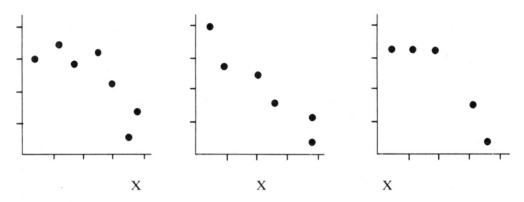

Here are the lines we drew. There is some room for disagreement but your lines should be similar to these.

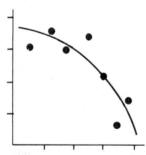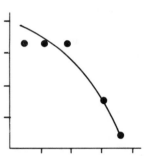

Some of the points are quite far from the line, but equal numbers are found on either side of the line.

All the points do not have to be equal distances from the line.

A straight line would have resulted in some points being a great distance from the line.

7. Now try again. Draw best-fit lines for the points on these graphs.

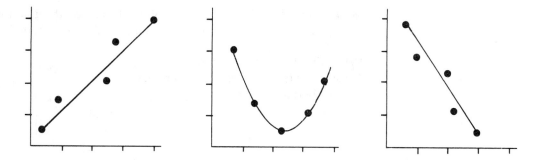

Be careful about "averaging out" the points. The number of points not on the line and their distance from the line should be approximately equal along both sides of the line.

You have just learned how to draw a line of best-fit. What you now have to learn to do is write a statement that describes the relationship between the variables on a graph.

For example, if you were given the graph on the right below, you should be able to write a statement as that found on the left.

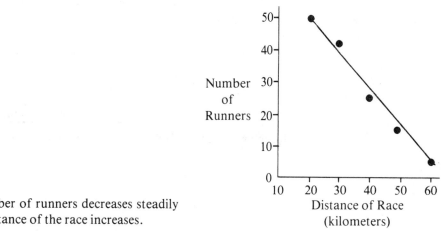

The number of runners decreases steadily as the distance of the race increases.

The rule for describing the relationship between variables on a graph is as follows:

Tell what happens to the responding variable *as* the manipulated variable changes.

For instance, a statement of relationship might read like this:

The temperature of water increases as the length of time it is heated increases.

8. Examine the following graph. Follow the line on the graph as it moves from left to right. Does the value of the responding variable increase or decrease?

INVESTIGATION: Ropes of different diameter are tested to see how much they will hold before breaking.

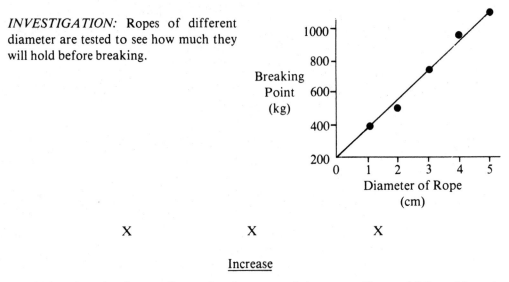

Breaking Point (kg)

Diameter of Rope (cm)

X   X   X

<u>Increase</u>

9. Using the rule given earlier, write the name of the responding variable and how it changes.

_____

X   X   X

<u>The breaking point increases.</u>

10. Now write "as" followed by the manipulated variable and how it changes.

_____

X   X   X

<u>As the diameter of the rope increases.</u>

You have now described the relationship between the two variables represented on the graph.

Try another one.

INVESTIGATION: The number of letters recognized on an eye chart was measured to see if it was affected by distance.

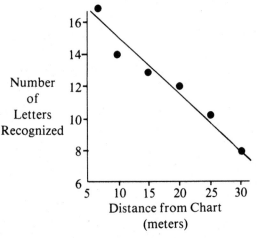

Number of Letters Recognized

Distance from Chart (meters)

11. What happens to the responding variable as the graph moves toward the right?

_____

X   X   X

<u>It decreases.</u>

12. Write the name of the responding variable and how it changes.

_____

X   X   X

<u>The number of letters recognized decreases.</u>

13. Follow this with "as" and the manipulated variable and how it changes.

_____

X   X   X

<u>As the distance from the chart increases.</u>

Two graphs are given below. Write a statement of the relationship between the variables for each group. Remember to use the rule.

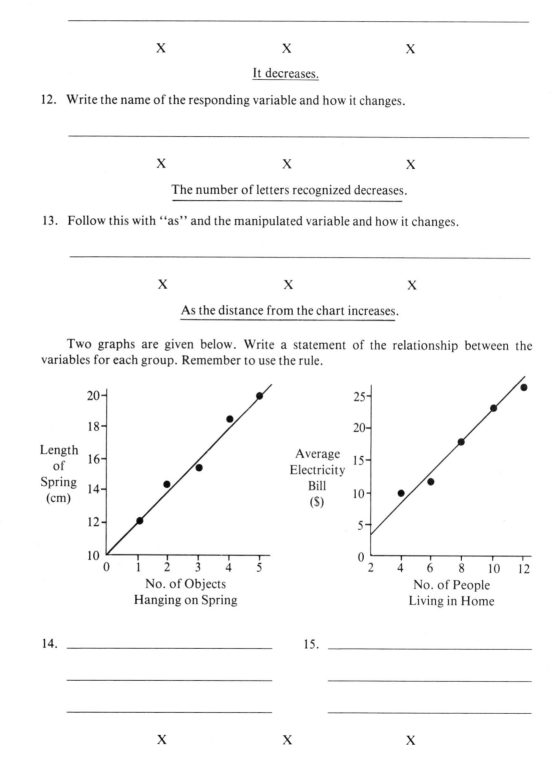

14. _____

_____

_____

15. _____

_____

_____

X   X   X

The length of a spring increases as the number of objects hanging from it increases.

The average electricity bill increased as the number of people living in the home increased.

The rules for describing the relationship between the variables on a *curved line* graph are as follows:

1. Describe the relationship in two sentences.
2. First describe the relationship until the curve changes direction.
3. Then tell what the relationship is for the rest of the graph.

For example, examine the curve at the right. The first sentence in the description should describe the section marked "1." The second sentence should describe the section marked "2."

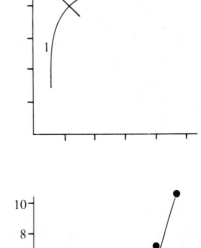

Examine the graph given below.

INVESTIGATION: An ice cube is placed in a glass of water and the temperature of the water is measured every few minutes.

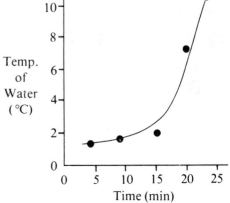

16. Place a mark across the best-fit line about where it first bends.

X   X   X

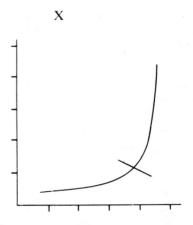

17. In one sentence describe what happens on the graph up until the mark you drew.

_____

X   X   X

The temperature of the water increased slowly as time passed.
Your statement does not have to be exactly the same as this but it should be similar.

18. Now describe what happens on the graph above the mark you drew.

_____

_____

X   X   X

After fifteen minutes the temperature of the water increased rapidly as time passed.
Together these two sentences should describe the entire graph.

Now try another.

INVESTIGATION: Tomato plants were grown at several different temperatures. The average number of tomatoes produced by each plant was measured.

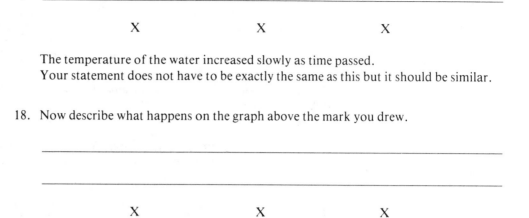

19. Mark where the best-fit line changes directions.

X   X   X

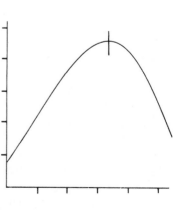

20. Describe what happens on the graph up until the mark you drew.

_____

_____

X   X   X

The average number of tomatoes produced increased rapidly until a temperature of 19 °C was reached.

21. Now describe what happens on the graph after the mark you drew.

_____

_____

X   X   X

Above 19 °C the average number of tomatoes produced declined rapidly.

INVESTIGATION: A pan of water is heated over a burner and the temperature is recorded every two minutes.

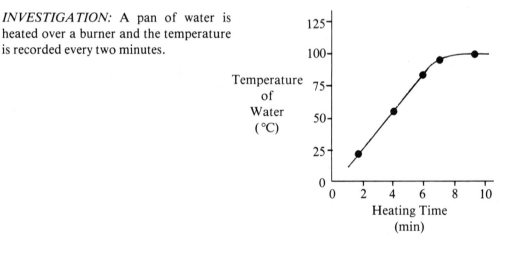

22. Write a statement of the relationship between the variables shown on the graph above.

_____

_____

X   X   X

The temperature of water steadily increases when heated up to 100 °C. After that the temperature stays about the same even though heating continues.

In the materials just completed you have learned to draw a best-fit line and write a statement of the relationship between the variables on a graph. In Chapter 9 you learned to construct a graph. Now you are going to get some practice problems in which you put all three of these skills together. However, before you do it on your own you will critique two problems in which someone else has made a graph and described it.

Two descriptions of investigations and the data collected from each are given below. Also given are a graph of the data, a best-fit line, and a statement of the relationship between the variables. You are to describe whether each has been properly prepared. If a section has not been correctly presented, check what part is wrong.

INVESTIGATION: The sea otters in a sheltered lagoon were counted over a number of years. These are the recorded data.

Year	Number of sea otters
1932	46
1940	42
1952	35
1962	30
1972	26

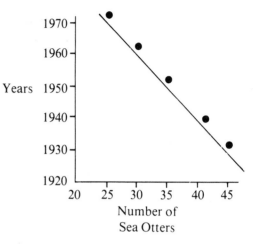

The number of sea otters in this location has been steadily decreasing since 1930.

23. Graph OK _____   Statement OK _____

_____   Variables on wrong axis   _____   Should be two sentences

_____   Numerical scale wrong   _____   Does not include both variables

_____   Number pairs in wrong position

Best-fit line OK _____

_____   Wrong shape line

_____   Line does not average points

          X   X   X

Statement is OK.
Variables on wrong axis.
Line does not average points (all the points are above the line).

INVESTIGATION: The average number of hits on a target in an archery contest were measured at different distances from the target.

Distance from target (meters)	Average number of hits
15	23
35	22
50	20
75	15
90	4

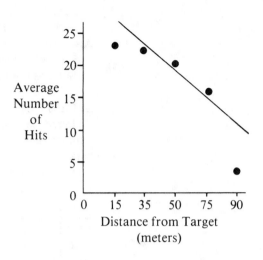

The average number of hits decreased steadily as the distance from the target increased.

24. Graph OK ____

____   Variables on wrong axis

____   Numerical scale wrong

____   Number pairs in wrong position

Best-fit line OK ____

____   Wrong shape line

____   Line does not average points

           X   X   X

Statement OK ____

____   Should be two sentences

____   Does not include both variables

Numerical scale wrong (intervals on horizontal axis are not of equal value).
Wrong shape best-fit line (should be a curved line).
Should be two sentences in the description.

You have now critiqued a couple of problems. Now you must put all the graphing skills you have learned to use.
Two descriptions of investigations and a table of data for each are given below. For each do the following:

a. Construct a graph of the data.
b. Draw a best-fit line.
c. Write a description of the relationship between the variables.

INVESTIGATION: A potato is cut in two and allowed to dry in the sun. The weight of the potato is measured as the days pass.

Elapsed time (days)	Weight of potato (grams)
1	330
7	300
12	180
14	150
21	160
26	120

25.

X   X   X

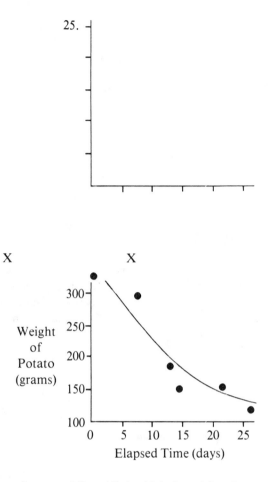

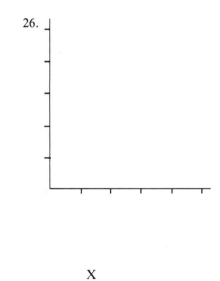

As the days pass, the weight of the potato drops rapidly until the 15th day. After that the weight loss is very slow and seems to be stopping.

INVESTIGATION: A fire chief is doing an analysis of his men at work. He measures the average time it takes a fireman to climb ladders of different lengths.

Length of ladder (m)	Time to climb (seconds)
1	2
2	5
3	8
8	18
12	22
15	53

26.

X   X   X

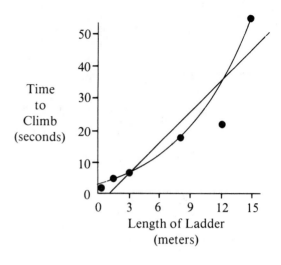

(**Note:** Either a curved or straight best-fit line could be used here.) As the length of the ladder increases the time to climb it steadily increases. (If you draw a curved line of best-fit you may want to add a second sentence like this one.) Above lengths of 12 meters the time to climb increases more rapidly.

If you were successful on the last two problems, you have learned some important skills that are helpful in solving science problems. In the part of the program you will study next, you will learn to acquire and process your own data.

Now take the self-test for Chapter 10.

Self-test for Chapter 10:

DESCRIBING RELATIONSHIPS BETWEEN VARIABLES

1. A description of an investigation and a table of data are given below.
   a. Construct a graph.
   b. Draw a best-fit line.
   c. Write a statement of the relationship between the variables.

   INVESTIGATION: An investigation was carried out to determine the relationship between the size of an automobile motor and the gasoline mileage.

Size of motor (horsepower)	Average kilometers per liter of gasoline
47	7
100	5
140	4
193	3.5
227	3

   _____

   _____

   _____

   _____

2. Draw a best-fit line for the points on the graph.

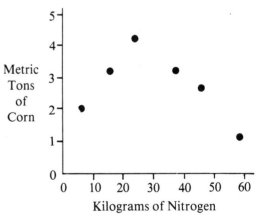

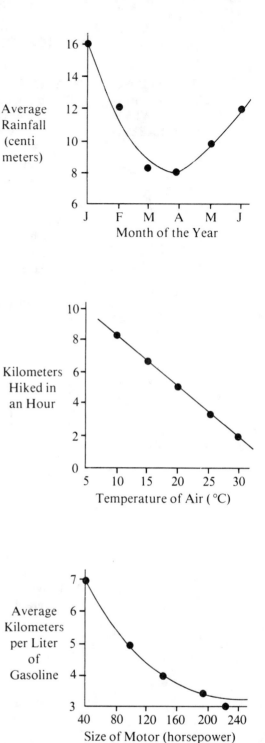

3. Write a statement of the relationship between the variables shown on this graph.

   INVESTIGATION: A weather station kept a record for a ten year period of the average amount of rainfall during several months.

   _____

   _____

   _____

   _____

4. Write a statement of the relationship between the variables shown on this graph.

   INVESTIGATION: Some soldiers were tested to see if the number of kilometers they could hike in an hour was affected by the temperature.

   _____

   _____

   _____

   _____

SELF-TEST ANSWERS: Describing Relationships Between Variables

1.

As the size of the motor increases, the number of kilometers per liter decreases. However, for motors above 120 horsepower, the decrease is slower.

2.

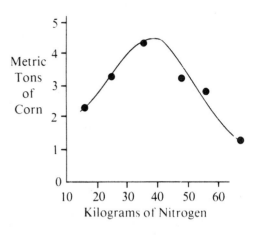

3. Between January and April the average rainfall per month steadily decreases. Between April and June the average rainfall per month steadily increases.
4. As the temperature of the air increases the number of kilometers marched in an hour by soldiers steadily decreases.

ACQUIRING AND PROCESSING YOUR OWN DATA 11

Purpose: In the past three chapters you have been working with many data tables. However, the number pairs in these data tables were produced by someone else. In this chapter you will carry out several investigations and produce your own tables of data.

Objectives: After studying this chapter you should be able to:

1. conduct an investigation and obtain a table of data.
2. construct a graph of the data and a statement of the relationship between the variables. (This task was introduced to you in Chapters 9 and 10.)

Approximate time for completion: 60 minutes

Note: In this chapter it is assumed that you know how to make measurements of mass, length, time-temperature, force, volume, and rate. If you are not sure that you know how to make these measurements, you may wish to review Chapter 4.

An experiment generally begins with a problem. Someone observes something occurring and wonders "Why?" For example, everyone knows that the old cliche, "a watched pot never boils," is not true; however, it does raise an interesting problem. What determines the rate at which water heats? Examine this problem a little closer. What are some of the variables that could affect the heating rate of water?

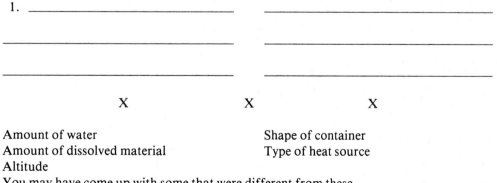

1. _____   _____

_____   _____

_____   _____

          X   X   X

Amount of water   Shape of container
Amount of dissolved material   Type of heat source
Altitude
You may have come up with some that were different from these.

If the variable, "amount of dissolved material," was selected for examination, one could make this hypothesis: The time required to change temperature increases as the amount of material dissolved in water increases. The first exercise of data gathering will be to conduct the experiment proposed to test this hypothesis. The equipment you need and the directions you are to follow are given below.

4 pyrex beakers (100 ml)
1 graduated cylinder
1 measuring spoon
1 burner support stand
1 alcohol burner
1 thermometer
1 timer
sugar

Activity 1   Label the beakers 0, 1, 2, and 3. Measure 50 ml of water into each. Dissolve one measure of sugar in beaker 1, 2 measures in beaker 2, and 3 in beaker 3. Place no sugar in beaker 0. Heat each beaker for three minutes. Record the change in temperature in the table below.

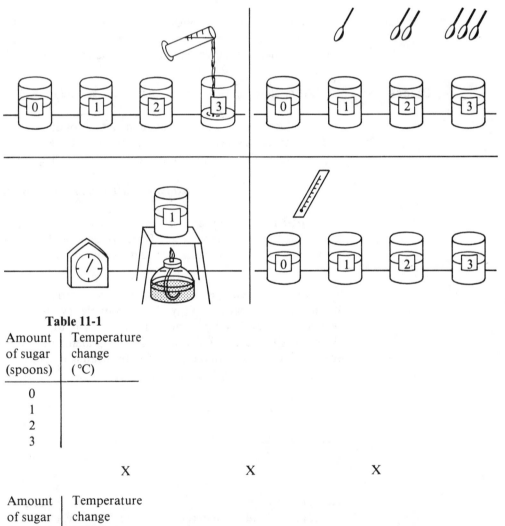

Table 11-1

Amount of sugar (spoons)	Temperature change (°C)
0	
1	
2	
3	

X   X   X

Amount of sugar (spoons)	Temperature change (°C)
0	38
1	35
2	32
3	31

These are data we collected.

2. Why did you use beaker 0?

_____

_____

X   X   X

To know that the sugar causes any change, it is necessary to know what happens when sugar is not present. More about such controls in Chapter 12.

3. Using the data obtained from your investigation, construct a graph and a statement about the relationship between the amount of dissolved sugar and the rate of temperature change.

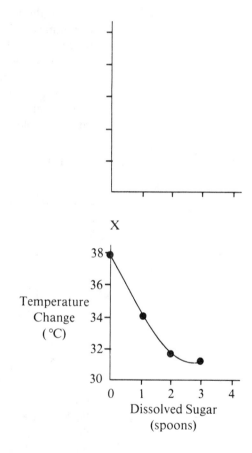

X   X   X

As the amount of dissolved sugar increases the temperature change decreases. The addition of more than two spoons of sugar results in no increase in temperature change.

Your statement may be different from this one if your graph differs.

This is a graph of the data collected earlier. Yours may be different because the data you gathered were different from ours.

Here is another practice exercise:

Bruce wanted to determine the relationship between the mass of an object and the force needed to overcome friction. He reasoned that in order to do this he would have to make sure that the texture and the amount of surface contact area remained the same under all conditions. Taking this and other things into consideration, he stated the following hypothesis: The greater the mass of an object, the greater the force needed to overcome friction.

Your second practice exercise will be to gather data to test this hypothesis. Collect the equipment listed below and follow the directions given.

1 wooden block   1 spring balance
2 baby food jars   1 graduated cylinder
                                  1 equal-arm balance
                                  a set of masses

Activity 2   Pull the wooden block along the surface of a table and record the force needed to keep it moving (not to start it). Add water to a baby food jar until the jar plus the water has a mass of 100 grams. Place this jar on the block and pull it again. Record this force in your data table. Add 100 grams of water to this jar and find the force needed to pull the block plus 200 grams. Now add a second jar containing water, with a mass of 100 grams and again find the force needed to pull the block with two jars on it. Add 100 grams of water to this jar and find the force needed to pull the block plus 400 grams. Complete the data table below and compare your findings with ours.

Table 11-2

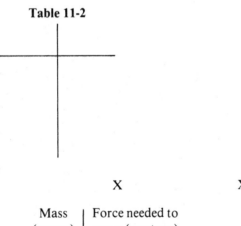

Mass (grams)	Force needed to move (newtons)
Block	.75
Block + 100	1.00
Block + 200	1.25
Block + 300	1.50
Block + 400	1.75

Because of the nature of the surface and the size of the block, your data table should differ only in the force column.

4. Why couldn't you use a heavier block instead of adding mass?

_____

_____

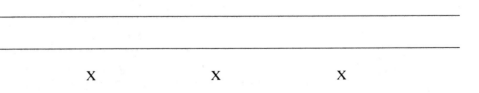

Using a different block could have changed the surface area and the texture of the surface, thereby adding other variables.

5. Using the data obtained from your investigation, construct a graph and a statement about the relationship between the mass of an object and the force needed to move the object.

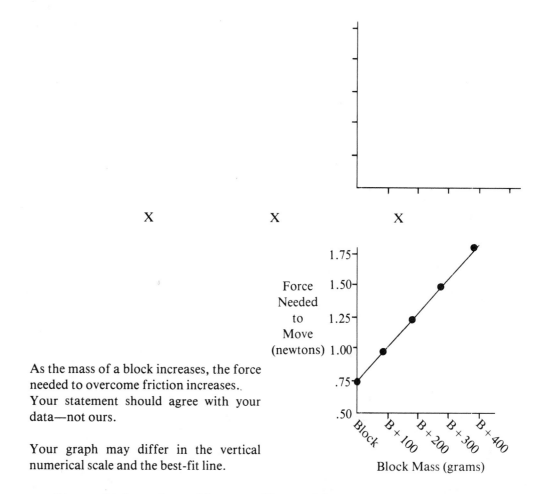

X   X   X

As the mass of a block increases, the force needed to overcome friction increases.
Your statement should agree with your data—not ours.

Your graph may differ in the vertical numerical scale and the best-fit line.

In your third practice problem you will use a siphon to empty a container. The data you gather are to be used to determine how the diameter of a siphon affects the time required to remove water from the container.

Assemble the equipment listed below and carry out the investigation as directed.

4 rubber tubes (each with a different inside diameter)
2 large containers
1 timer

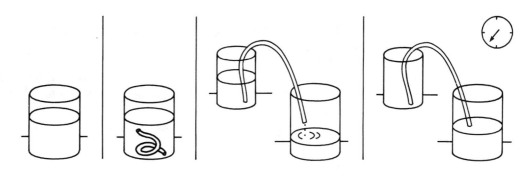

Activity 3   Fill one container to any level (as long as it is the same each time). Submerge the entire tube in the water and pinch one end closed. Pull that end out and down the side until it is below the bottom of the beaker. Release the pinch and record the time required to empty the beaker. Repeat for each tube. Record all your data in the data table below. Construct a graph and a statement of the relationship between the variables from the data obtained.

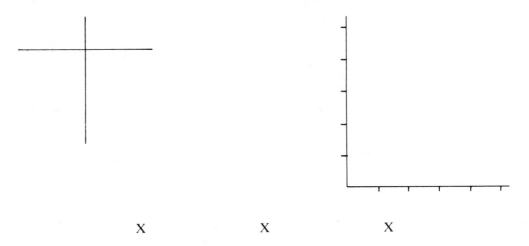

X   X   X

These are the data gathered during the investigation when we did it. You can compare your results with ours. Remember that the data you obtain and the graph you make may differ from ours and yet be correct. One difference might be in the amount of water—we used 300 ml.

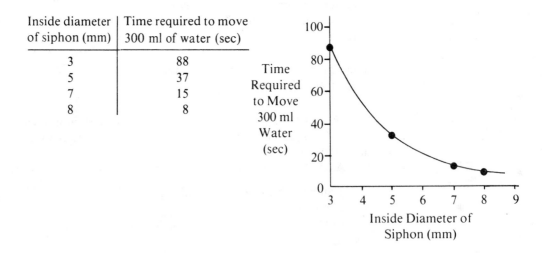

Inside diameter of siphon (mm)	Time required to move 300 ml of water (sec)
3	88
5	37
7	15
8	8

The time required to siphon water decreases rapidly as the inside diameter of the tube increased to about 7 mm. Above this, the time required to remove the water decreased very slowly.

You have now carried out a few investigations. In the following chapter you will examine parts of an investigation with the hopes that you will later be able to design investigations.

Now turn to the next page and take the self-test.

Self-test for Chapter 11:

**ACQUIRING AND
PROCESSING
YOUR OWN DATA**

1. You are interested in determining the relationship between the amount of exercise an individual does and his pulse rate. To collect some data on this relationship carry out the following investigation.

   Sit quietly for about 5 minutes and then count your number of heartbeats for 15 seconds. Now quickly step up onto a stool 5 times. Count your heartbeat for 15 seconds. Rest until your pulse rate returns to the resting rate. Quickly step up onto the stool 10 times. Count your heartbeat for 15 seconds. Repeat this procedure for 15, 20, and 25 step-ups.

   Construct a graph and a statement of the relationship between the variables for the data you gather.

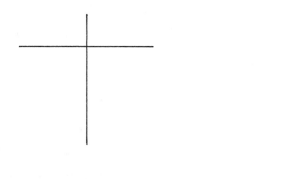
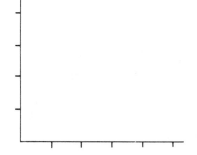

**SELF-TEST
ANSWERS:
Acquiring and
Processing
Your Own Data**

Here are the data gathered from an investigation we carried out. Your data will almost certainly be different.

Number of step-ups	Heartbeats (/15 sec)
0	20
5	26
10	28
15	32
20	36
25	39

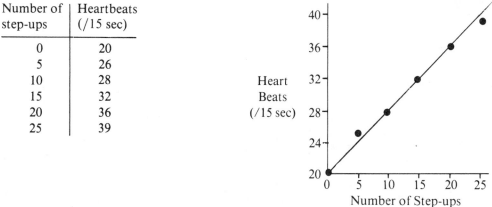

The pulse rate increases as the number of step-ups increase.

ANALYZING
INVESTIGATIONS 12

Purpose: Before you can design your own investigations, you need to learn to recognize the parts of a typical investigation. What are the variables under study? What hypothesis is being tested? These and other questions can be answered by analyzing an investigation.

Objectives: After studying this chapter you should be able to:

1. identify the manipulated, responding, and controlled variables in an experiment.
2. identify the hypothesis being tested when supplied with a description of an investigation.

Approximate time for completion: 30 minutes

There are many factors which might affect the outcome of an experiment, factors that the experimenter may not be interested in at the moment. For example, suppose we wanted to test this situation.

The greater the amount of light,
  the taller a plant will grow.

We could grow some plants in bright light and others where the light is dim. However, any results obtained would be worthless if the amount of water each group received was different or if they were potted in different soils.

Perhaps now you are beginning to see one of the problems with investigations. We want to be able to say that the manipulated variable *and only the manipulated variable* affected the responding variable. We must make sure, therefore, that any other factor that could have an affect is prevented from doing so.

A variable that might affect an experiment but is kept from doing so is called a *controlled variable.* An experiment using such a variable is said to be controlled.

We could then define a *controlled variable* as one that is prevented from affecting outcome of an experiment.

What variables are being controlled in this experiment?

Place six cups of water in each of four identical coffee makers. Add one teaspoon of coffee to the first pot, two to the second, three to the third, and four to the last. Brew each batch of coffee for ten minutes.

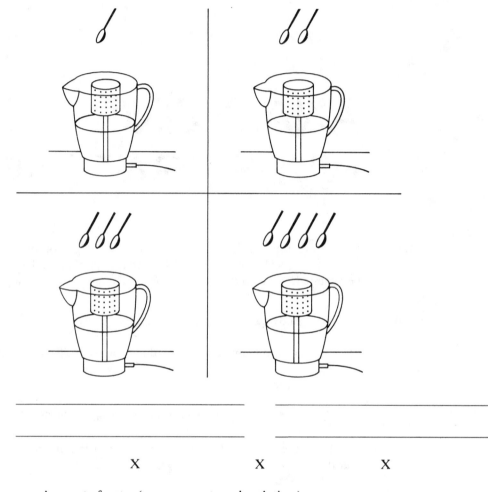

X   X   X

Amount of water (same amount used each time)
Coffee maker (identical coffee makers used)
Brewing time (each brewed same amount of time)
Coffee (same kind of coffee used in each pot)

You may have listed other controlled variables besides these. Notice that the manipulated variable in this experiment is the amount of coffee. If different amounts of water were used in each pot it would not be possible to say that the outcome was due only to the amount of coffee used.

What factors are being controlled in this next experimental setup?

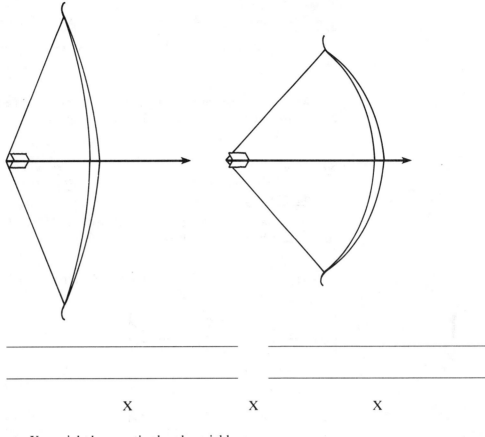

_____   _____

_____   _____

X   X   X

You might have noticed such variables as:

Length of arrow   Weight of arrow
Type of point   Strength of bow
Size of arrow   Temperature of air
Shape of feathers   Density of air
Length of bow

Actually you can not be sure about these because you only have a picture to examine.

What variables are being controlled in the following experiment?

A flock of Leghorn chickens is divided into two groups. Both groups are housed in the same building, fed at the same time each day, and get the same amount of water. One group gets Brand X feed and the other Brand Y.

_____   _____

_____   _____

X   X   X

<u>Type of chicken</u>   <u>Feeding time</u>
<u>Type of housing</u>   <u>Amount of water</u>

If you went beyond this list you have expressed variables that were not *explicitly* presented.

What additional variables are probably being controlled in the previous experiment even though they are not mentioned in the description?

X   X   X

<u>Size of each group</u>   <u>Nesting characteristics</u>
<u>Temperature of housing</u>   <u>Roosting characteristics</u>
<u>Amount of feed available</u>

This time you may have come up with others. This is all right if you believe that they could affect the responding variable.

What variables are being controlled in this experimental setup?

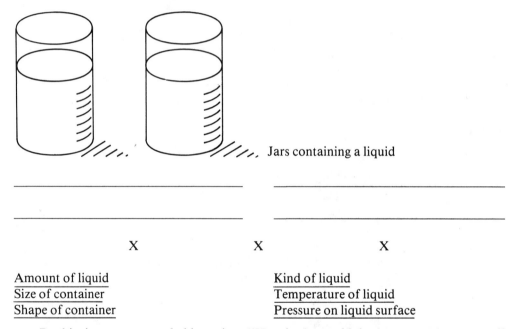 Jars containing a liquid

_____   _____

_____   _____

X   X   X

<u>Amount of liquid</u>   <u>Kind of liquid</u>
<u>Size of container</u>   <u>Temperature of liquid</u>
<u>Shape of container</u>   <u>Pressure on liquid surface</u>

By this time you are probably saying, "How in the world do they expect me to get all of those. Besides I thought of some that they didn't." That is just the point. In any experiment there could be so many variables that need to be controlled no one could think of them all. The best way to make sure that all such variables are controlled is to make several experimental setups, each of which is treated exactly the same except for the manipulated variable.

An experiment designed to test the prediction:

The greater the amount of light,
the taller a plant will grow.

could be controlled by doing the following:

a.   All the plants are the *same* size
b.   The *same* soil in each pot
c.   Watered at the *same* time each day
d.   Given the *same* amount of water
e.   Kept in the *same* place

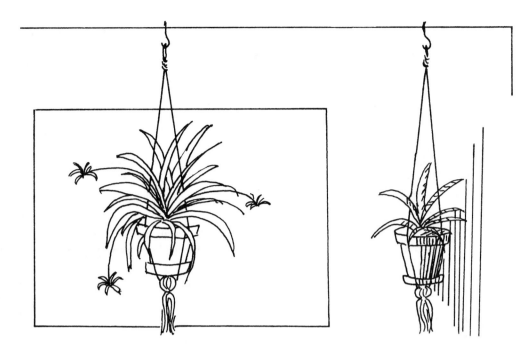

There would be one thing that is done differently. One group of plants would receive more light than the others. All other variables would be controlled by keeping them the *same* for each group of plants.

Suppose in this experiment that one group of plants was grown at 16 °C. What temperature would you keep the other group of plants?

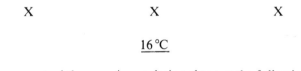

X   X   X

<u>16 °C</u>

How would you control the experiment designed to test the following hypothesis?

The greater the amount of salt added to ice, the lower the temperature of the mixture.

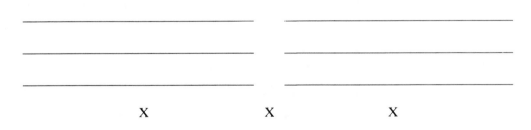

_____   _____

_____   _____

_____   _____

X   X   X

Several identical containers were filled with the *same amount of ice.* Use the *same kind of salt* in each and measure the temperature with the *same kind of thermometer* in each.
You may have thought of others. As long as you were attempting to keep everything in all setups the same except the amount of salt, it would be okay.

So far in this program you have learned to identify controlled variables. A controlled variable is something, other than the manipulated variable, that could affect the responding variable. In a controlled experiment the controlled variables are prevented from affecting the outcome by making sure they are the same in all cases.

A scientist is interested in explaining events. To do so he conducts investigations to determine what effect manipulated variables have on responding variables. In order to plan what investigations to carry out, a statement called a *hypothesis* is made. A hypothesis is a guess about the effect a manipulated variable will have on a responding variable.

What two variables will you find included in a hypothesis?

_____   _____

X   X   X

<u>Manipulated variable</u>   <u>Responding variable</u>

We could define a hypothesis as an attempt to predict an outcome.
Which of the following are stated as hypotheses?

_____ 1. As more salt is dissolved in water, the water becomes cloudy.

_____ 2. The earth's crust contains 90 elements.

_____ 3. Magnetism and gravity are not the same.

_____ 4. If the length of a vibrating string is increased, the sound will become louder.

X   X   X

<u>1,4</u>

Remember, a hypothesis is stated as the predicted effect one variable will have on another.

Which of these statements are hypotheses?

_____ 1. As the temperature of its environment increases, the temperature of a cold-blooded animal increases.

_____ 2. Glass is harder than iron; therefore glass will scratch anything which is softer than iron.

_____ 3. A change in weather causes a change in mood.

X   X   X

<u>1,2,3</u>

In all three cases we are predicting what will happen to a responding variable if we can manipulate another variable.

Which of these is stated as a hypothesis?

_____ 1. If clouds act as insulators, then the earth should get colder on cloudless nights.

_____ 2. Leaves manufacture food, stems transfer food, and roots store the food in plants. plants.

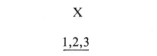

X   X   X

<u>1</u>

In #1 the effect of a manipulated variable (amount of cloud cover) on a responding variable (night time temperature) is predicted or hypothesized. Therefore, #1 is a hypothesis.

In #2, only results are reported. It, therefore, is not a hypothesis.

Which of these are hypotheses?

_____ 1. The colder the temperature, the slower plants grow.

_____ 2. The deeper one dives, the greater the pressure.

_____ 3. Algae are living organisms.

X   X   X

<u>1,2</u>

One could manipulate the temperature or the depth of the dive but there is no variable to manipulate in #3.

Remember that a hypothesis states what affect a manipulated variable will have on a responding variable.

Now you try to write a hypothesis. Write a statement that predicts the outcome if the *amount of light* is one variable and the other is *plant growth*.

_____

X   X   X

The *(greater, lesser)* the amount of light, the
(greater, lesser) the amount of plant growth.

This is only one of several you could have written if you tried to predict what would happen to one variable if you manipulated another. Remember that you don't have to know for sure what the effect will be, you're only making a guess. But remember, if you try to test your *hypothesis* it will be necessary to make sure that only one variable could cause the effect. You must *control* all other variables.

You now have had some practice in identifying variables and hypotheses when given the parts of an investigation. Next you will analyze the entire investigation and identify the variables involved and the hypothesis being tested.

Here is the description of an investigation:

John was interested in determining the affect the number of plants in an area has on growth rate. He planted radish seeds in several milk cartons. In the first carton, he planted 5 seeds 1 cm deep and no less than 5 cm apart, in the second, 10 seeds were planted 1 cm deep and no more than 2 cm apart, in the third, 15 seeds 1 cm deep and 1 cm apart, and in the fourth, 20 seeds 1 cm deep and 1/2 cm apart. Each carton was watered daily and daily measurements of the length of leaves were made.

What were some of the controlled variables? _____

_____

_____

What variable was manipulated? _____

Which variable was expected to respond? _____

What was the hypothesis being tested? _____

X   X   X

Some of the variables that were controlled are: Kind of seed; planting depth; soil; temperature; amount of water; kind of containers; and light received. Since the number of plants in an area was manipulated and the length of the leaves was expected to respond, the hypothesis probably reads: *As the number of plants in an area increases, the length of the leaves will become shorter.* Or it could have predicted that the leaves would be longer. In stating a hypothesis the decision as to what the effect will be can be based on data gathered in related situations or it can be an out and out guess. Until data are gathered and interpreted, however, one guess is just as valid as another.

Here is a description of another experiment:

Is there a relationship between the amount of training received and the length of time a learned behavior persists in insects? Select a number of sowbugs which always turn right when entering the intersection of a T-shaped maze. Using the tendency of sowbugs to avoid light, it is possible to train them to turn left by shining a strong-light from the right as they enter the intersection. Subject an animal to 1, 5, 10, 15, or 20 training sessions. Test each animal once an hour by running it through the T-maze.

What variables were being controlled in this investigation?

_____   _____

_____   _____

_____   _____

What variable was being manipulated? _____

What variable was expected to respond? _____

X   X   X

Type of animal   Light source
Maze   Temperature

These are just some of the controlled variables. You may have stated others.

The amount of training was being manipulated, and the length of time the training persists was expected to respond.

Sometimes it is possible to make inferences concerning variables and hypotheses given only the physical setup and the problem under study. Examine the stated problem and drawings below and answer the questions that follow.

Problem: Will different kinds of soil retain different amounts of water?

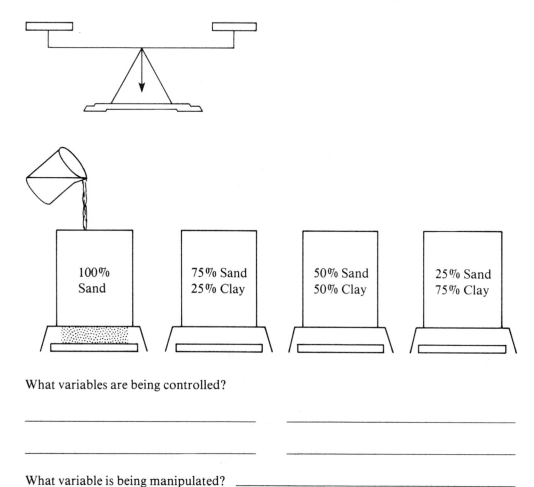

What variables are being controlled?

_____   _____

_____   _____

What variable is being manipulated? _____

What variable is expected to respond? _____

What hypothesis is being tested? _____

X   X   X

Such variables as the amount of soil, size of container, temperature, and kind of sand or clay are being controlled. The amount of sand (clay) in the soil is being manipulated and the weight of water retained is expected to respond. The hypothesis most likely being tested is: The amount of water retained by the soil increases as the amount of sand in the soil decreases.

You now have had some practice in analyzing investigations, looking at the variables involved and identifying the hypothesis being tested. In the next section you will begin the task of designing your own investigation. Among other things this requires you to construct hypotheses.

Now take the self-test for Chapter 12.

Self-test for Chapter 12:

ANALYZING INVESTIGATIONS

Read the description of this investigation and then answer the questions below.

1. A study was done of the concentration of bleach needed to change the color of cloth. Squares of cloth were soaked in a bleach solution for five minutes each. Concentrations of 100, 95, 90, 85, . . ., 5, and 0% bleach were used.
   a. Identify the controlled variables in the above investigation.
   b. Identify the manipulated variable.
   c. Identify the responding variable.
   d. State the hypothesis being tested.

   a. _____
   b. _____
   c. _____
   d. _____
   _____

2. Check each of the statements below that is stated as a hypothesis.
   a. The rusty nail in the board is four inches long.
   b. The lighter the balloon, the higher it will climb.
   c. Plants grow toward light.
   d. The more water in a tomato, the firmer it will be.

   a. _____
   b. _____
   c. _____
   d. _____

3. Classify these statements as hypotheses (H) or non-hypotheses (N):
   a. Solids will dissolve faster than gases.
   b. There are no caves in Kansas.
   c. The larger the surface area, the faster the evaporation.
   d. A tomato is 96% water.

   N   H
   N   H
   N   H
   N   H

4. Suppose you wished to test the hypothesis stated below. Which of the variables listed should be controlled in the experiment?
   Hypothesis: The more water a plant receives, the larger it will grow.
   a. amount of water
   b. kind of plants
   c. potting soil
   d. amount of light

   a. _____
   b. _____
   c. _____
   d. _____

5. List four variables you would control if you were to test this hypothesis.
Hypothesis: The greater the horsepower, the faster the car will travel.

_____

_____

_____

_____

_____

SELF-TEST ANSWERS: Analyzing Investigations

1. a.   type of bleach, size of cloth, kind of cloth, amount of bleach solution
   b.   concentration of bleach
   c.   color of cloth
   d.   the greater the concentration of bleach the greater the change in color of the cloth
2. b,d
3. a. H   b. N   c. H   d. N
4. b,c,d
5. weight of car
   type of gasoline
   size of car
   type of transmission

Your answers may vary greatly. Consider them correct if they deal with the characteristics of the car or its environment.

CONSTRUCTING HYPOTHESES 13

Purpose:　　Hypotheses are *guesses* about the relationships between variables. Before any sensible investigating or experimenting is done a hypothesis is usually stated. The hypothesis provides guidance to an investigator about what data to collect. In this chapter you will learn to construct or write hypotheses. This skill will be used later (Chapters 15 and 16) when you plan and carry out your own investigations.

Objective:　　After studying this chapter you should be able to:

1. construct a hypothesis when provided with a problem.

Approximate time for completion: 25 minutes

The first difficulty when constructing a hypothesis is to identify variables that could possibly affect the responding variable. To do this you can examine the object in a problem and the *environment* of that object. For example, consider this problem:

What affects how fast a person can run the 100 meter dash?

There are factors related both to the *individual* and to the *environment* of the individual which could affect his speed. For example, lung capacity, muscle tone, length of legs, and motivation are characteristics of an individual which could affect his speed. The direction and speed of the wind, surface of the track, and type of shoes worn are characteristics of an individual's environment which could affect his speed.

Here is a problem for you to analyze. First, consider variables related to the object, then consider variables related to the environment of the object.

Problem: How fast will an object fall through a liquid?

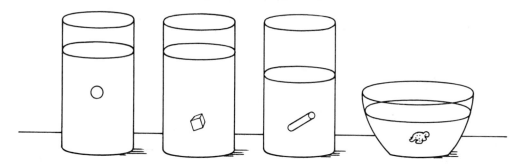

What characteristics of the *object* might affect the speed as it falls through the liquid? List some of them.

_____   _____

_____   _____

X   X   X

volume of the object   weight of the object
shape of the object   density of the object

These are just a few. There are many others.

What characteristics of the environment of a object might affect its speed as it falls through the liquid? List some possibilities.

_____   _____

_____   _____

X   X   X

Both the liquid and the container are part of the environment of the object so characteristics of either could have an effect.

Liquid   **Container**
temperature of liquid   size of container
amount of liquid   shape of container

Only some of the possibilities are listed. You may have come up with others.

Another problem for you to analyze is given below. You are to identify some variables which might affect the rate of growth of the plants. Remember to consider characteristics of both the plant and its environment.

Problem: What affects the rate at which a plant grows?

List some variables which might affect the rate of growth.

_____   _____

_____   _____

_____   _____

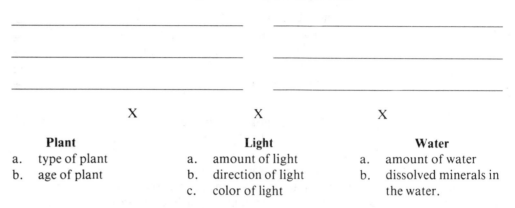

	X		X		X

Plant	**Light**	**Water**
a. type of plant	a. amount of light	a. amount of water
b. age of plant	b. direction of light	b. dissolved minerals in
	c. color of light	the water.

The list of possibilities is almost endless. Only a few are shown here.

Another problem for you to analyze is given below. This time identify some variables that might affect the exercise time.

Problem: What determines the amount of time an animal will spend in an exercise wheel?

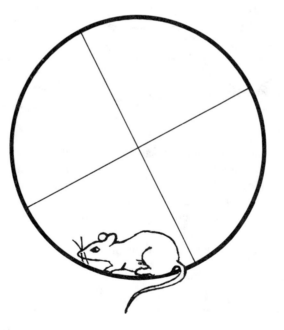

List some variables that might affect the exercise time.

Animal	**Environment of animal**
_____	_____
_____	_____
_____	_____
X	X	X

	Animal	**Food**	**Cage**

Animal

a. age of animal
b. sex of animal
c. number of legs on animal

The list could go on and on.

Food

a. amount of food
b. feeding time
c. type of food

Cage

a. size of cage
b. shape of cage

Once the variable of interest has been selected, a testable hypothesis can be stated. The term "testable hypothesis" is used because this indicates one of the functions a hypothesis should serve. A hypothesis should point the way towards the design of an investigation to test it. To construct a hypothesis, express what you think will be the effect of the variable you will manipulate on the variable you expect to respond. This guess can be based on fact, opinion, hunch, or whatever sources you may possess. For example, to construct a hypothesis related to the problem, "What affects the speed of a car?," one might select the variable "size of tires" to test. One could then construct a hypothesis in the following way: as the size of its tires *increases,* the speed of a car *decreases.*

In the problem below, construct a hypothesis for each variable selected for testing by predicting its effect on the hatching rate.

Problem: Russell raises bees. He noticed that varying numbers of young hatched from the same number of hives at different times. He wondered what factors might influence the hatching rate of the bees. He selected the following variables to be tested:

a. temperature of the hive
b. relative humidity inside the hive
c. amount of food available
d. number of bees living in the hive

Construct a hypothesis for each variable listed above.

a. _____

_____

b. _____

_____

c. _____

_____

d. _____

_____

X   X   X

a. As the temperature of the hive *increases,* the hatching rate *will increase.*
b. As the relative humidity inside the hive *increases,* the hatching rate *will decrease.*
c. As the amount of food available *decreases,* the hatching rate *increases.*
d. As the number of bees living in the hive *increases,* the hatching rate *decreases.*

Your guess as to the effect of each variable is as good as ours. It will remain just that—a guess, until someone tests it.

Problem: What factors determine the rate at which an object falls through air?

Possible variables: a.   volume of object
                     b.   surface area of object
                     c.   length of fall
                     d.   weight of object

Construct a hypothesis for each variable.

a.   _____

     _____

b.   _____

     _____

c. _____

_____

d. _____

_____

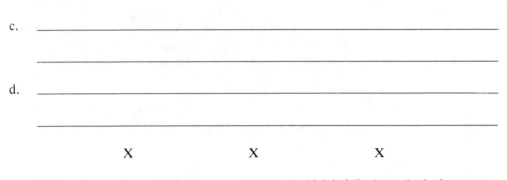

a. As the volume of an object *increases,* the rate at which it falls through air *decreases.*
b. As the surface area of an object *increases,* the rate of falling through air *decreases.*
c. The longer (or farther) an object falls through air, the faster it will fall.
d. The more weight an object has, the faster it will fall through air.

Your hypotheses may be entirely different from those above and still be correct. In each case, however, your statement should include the predicted effect of a manipulated variable on a responding variable.

Now you will practice putting together the skills on which you have been working. You will be presented with several problem situations. You will be expected to identify variables and construct hypotheses.

Identify a list of possible variables and construct at least three hypotheses related to the problem given below.

Problem: Why is it warmer in one house than another?

a. _____

_____

_____

b. _____

_____

_____

c. _____

_____

_____

        X   X   X

a.   *outside temperature*

The higher the outside temperature, the higher the temperature inside the house.

b.   *location of house*

The nearer the house is to the equator, the higher the temperature inside the house.

c.   *slope of roof*
The steeper the roof, the higher the temperature inside the house.

d.   *thickness of insulation*
The thicker the insulation, the higher the temperature inside the house.

e.   *number of openings to the outside*
The more openings (window and doors) to the outside, the lower the temperature inside the house.

These are only a few of the many possible hypotheses that could be constructed concerning this problem. Your hypotheses may be very different from these.

Here is another problem. Generate a list of possible variables and construct at least three hypotheses related to the length of a shadow.

Problem: What factors determine the length of a shadow?

a.   _____

_____

_____

b.   _____

_____

_____

c.   _____

_____

_____

X   X   X

a.   *height of object*
The taller an object, the longer its shadow.
b.   *time of day*
The closer the time moves toward noon, the shorter the shadow of an object.
c.   *season of year*
As the season progresses from summer to winter, the length of a shadow becomes longer.

You have now had an opportunity to construct several hypotheses. A second task required in order to design an investigation is to decide how you will measure those variables you have selected to test. This measurement problem will be taken up in the next chapter. Finally, in the last two chapters you will really "put it all together" and use skills learned in these chapters to design and conduct some investigations.

Now take the self-test for Chapter 13.

Self-test for Chapter 13:

For each of the following problems list three variables which could affect the responding variable. State a hypothesis for each variable listed.

1. Why doesn't an animal breathe at the same rate all the time?

Variable 1 _____

Hypothesis 1 _____

Variable 2 _____

Hypothesis 2 _____

Variable 3 _____

Hypothesis 3 _____

2. What determines how high a balloon will rise?

Variable 1 _____

Hypothesis 1 _____

Variable 2 _____

Hypothesis 2 _____

Variable 3 _____

Hypothesis 3 _____

**SELF-TEST
ANSWERS:
Constructing
Hypotheses**

1. Here are a few of the many possible variables. Included with each is a possible hypothesis. Your answers may be different and still be correct.

amount of exercise

As the amount of exercise increases, the breathing rate will increase.

age of the animal

As the age of the animal increases, the breathing rate will not change.

temperature of environment

As the temperature of the environment decreases, the breathing rate will increase.

body size

As an animal's body size increases, the breathing rate increases.

altitude

As the altitude increases, the animal's breathing rate increases.

2. *size of balloon*

The larger a balloon is, the higher it will rise.

weight of balloon

The lighter a balloon is, the higher it will rise.

temperature of air

The cooler the air surrounding the balloon, the higher it will rise.

temperature of balloon

The warmer the balloon, the higher it will rise.

DEFINING VARIABLES OPERATIONALLY 14

Purpose: During an investigation measurements of the variables are made. However, before making the measurements the investigator must decide *how* to measure each variable. In this chapter you will practice making decisions about how to measure variables.

Objectives: When you finish this chapter you should be able to:

1. state how the variables are operationally defined in an investigation when given a description of the investigation.
2. construct operational definitions for variables.

Approximate time for completion: 25 minutes

By selecting a procedure for measuring a variable you are making an operational definition. To operationally define a variable means to decide how you will measure it. Thus an operational definition is a made-up definition.

Different investigators may use different operational definitions for the same variable. For example, suppose an investigation was being conducted to test the effects of Vitamin E on the "endurance of a person." The variable "endurance of a person" could be defined many different ways:

a.   the number of hours a person could stay awake
b.   the distance a person could run without stopping
c.   the number of jumping jacks a person could do before tiring

Each of the above statements is an operational definition of the same variable.

Here is a brief description of an investigation. Your job is to determine how each of the variables was operationally defined in this investigation. That is, you are to say how the manipulated and responding variables in this investigation were measured.

Investigation: A study was done to determine if safety advertising had any effect on automobile accidents. Different numbers of billboards were put up in Cleveland over a period of four months to see if the number of people hospitalized because of auto accidents was affected. In March, five billboards carried safety messages; in April there were ten; in May there were fifteen; and in June there were twenty. During each of these four months, a record of the number of people hospitalized because of accidents was measured.

The variable *safety advertising* was manipulated in this investigation to see if *automobile accidents* would respond. How was each one operationally defined?

Safety advertising _____

_____

Automobile accidents_____

_____

X   X   X

Safety advertising is operationally defined as the number of safety billboards (what was observed) put up in the city (what operation was performed) during each month.

Automobile accidents are operationally defined as the number of people (what is observed) who are hospitalized (what operation was performed) because of automobile accidents.

It is important to note that these variables, or any others, could be measured in a variety of ways. It is entirely up to the investigator how the variables in his study will be operationally defined. However, the operational definition should be explicit enough that another person could carry out the measurement without any further aid from the investigator.

Now take a look at this investigation. How were the manipulated and responding variables operationally defined in this study?

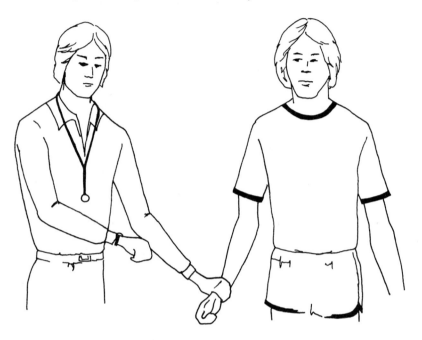

Investigation: A study was done to determine the effect that exercise has on pulse rate. High school students did different numbers of jumping jacks and then their pulse rate was measured. One group did ten, a second group did twenty, a third group did thirty, and a fourth group did forty jumping jacks. Following the exercise the pulse rate was immediately measured by counting the pulse for one minute.

How was each variable operationally defined in this investigation?

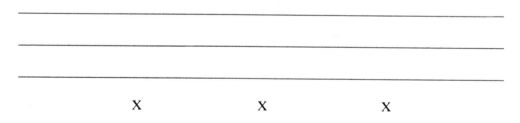

X   X   X

"Amount of exercise" is the manipulated variable. It was measured by counting the number of (what was observed) jumping jacks (the operation performed) a person had done. "Pulse rate" is the responding variable. It was measured by counting the number of heartbeats felt at the wrist (what was observed) following exercise (the operation performed).

Amount of exercise and pulse rate could have been operationally defined in other ways. For example, "amount of exercise" could have been defined by having the students run in place for designated periods of time. It could have been operationally defined in terms of the number of knee bends each student did. The point to be made is that "amount of exercise" can be defined any way you want to in an experiment. There are a variety of ways you could define it. When you select one way to measure "amount of exercise" for your experiment, you have defined it operationally.

Here is a third investigation. Read it and write down how the manipulated and responding variables were operationally defined in this study.

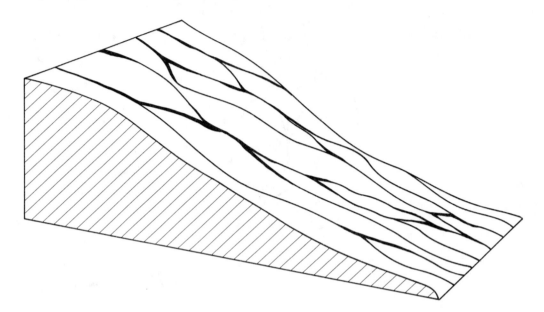

Investigation: A study was conducted to see if the amount of erosion was affected by the slope of the land. The end of a stream table was raised to four different heights (10 cm, 20 cm, 30 cm, 40 cm) in order to make it slope different amounts. (A stream table is a plastic box about 40 cm wide and 100 cm long. Sand or soil is placed in the box and water can be run in at one end.) At each height a liter of water was poured in at one end of the stream table. After the water had run over the soil, the depth of the gulley cut by the water was measured.

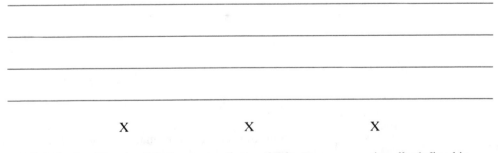

X   X   X

"Amount of erosion" is the responding variable. It was operationally defined in this study as the depth of (the observation) the gulley cut (the performance) by the water. "Slope of the land," the manipulated variable, was operationally defined as the height (the observation) to which the end of the stream table was raised (the performance).

Clearly, these two variables could have been operationally defined in other ways. For example, "slope of the land" could be measured in degrees of tilt of the box. Measuring the mass of the eroded soil would be another way of operationally defining "amount of erosion."

To get you to think of a variety of ways that a variable might be operationally defined, consider this case. Suppose you wanted to operationally define the variable "size of a person." Write down at least three ways this variable could be defined operationally.

_____

_____

_____

_____

X   X   X

Here are some ways we thought of that could be used to define the "size of a person":

a. the reading in kilograms obtained when a person steps on a scale

b. the smallest number showing when a person stands against a ruler which extends from the floor up

c. the amount of water that overflows when a person is submerged in a full bathtub

d. the amount of tape required to encircle the chest, waist, and hips

Now try another variable. Suppose you are an expert in agriculture and you are growing beans in an experiment. You need to operationally define the variable "amount of plant growth." Write down three different ways that you could operationally define this variable. Just think of three different ways you could measure how much the plant grew.

_____

_____

_____

X   X   X

Some possibilities you might have thought of are:

Count the number of leaves on a plant. Wait two weeks and count them again.

Measure the distance from the soil to the uppermost leaf. Ten days later, measure it again.

Weigh the plant and its pot. Wait one month and do it again. The difference is how much it grew.

Suppose that an elementary school has a program underway for the purpose of increasing students' "enjoyment of reading." What are some of the different ways that "enjoyment of reading" could be operationally defined? List at least three ways. Try to think of some specific things you could measure with your students in your classroom that would indicate their "enjoyment of reading."

_____

_____

_____

X   X   X

You might attempt to measure the variable "enjoyment of reading" in some of these ways:

a. amount of time students voluntarily spend at the reading table

b. number of references to books read during sharing time

c. number of voluntary book reports

d. number of books taken home

Some of these operational definitions may appeal more to you than others. If you were doing the experiment, of course, you could select the one you wished.

You probably realize by now that most operational definitions would not be found in the dictionary. Instead they have to be made up by the person who will use them. When you carry out an investigation, you have to decide how to measure the variables. When you do this, you are constructing operational definitions.

In the last part of this unit, you will be given three more variables to operationally define. For each you should try to think of a variety of ways to operationally define the variable.

Variable 1: Concern for Environment

Suppose that one of the goals of Springhill Elementary School is that all children acquire a "concern for their environment." What are some of the ways that they might operationally define this variable? Describe at least three.

_____

_____

_____

_____

X   X   X

Some possibilities are:

a.   the number of special projects students choose to do on environmental matters
b.   the pounds of trash picked up on the playground each week
c.   the number of brown bags thrown away (instead of reused) from the lunch room
d.   the number of paper towels used in the washrooms
e.   the number of posters on environmental matters in a "show-your-concern-with-a-poster" contest

Obviously there would be many ways the variable "concern for environment" could be operationally defined. The list provided is only suggestive. Very likely you had different and possibly better ideas.

Variable 2: Understanding of Fractions

Suppose that you are a fifth grade teacher and you want your students to "understand fractions." What are some of the ways that you might operationally define this variable? Describe at least three.

_____

_____

_____

_____

X   X   X

Some possibilities are:

In each case it is assumed that the student will be given the opportunity (the operation you perform) to demonstrate (what you observe) "understanding."

a. Add fractions.
b. Represent portions of a cut-up object with fractions.
c. Select numbers that are fractions from a list.
d. Reduce fractions to lowest terms.

These are a few of the ways that you might operationally define "understanding of fractions" for a fifth grader. In each of the above it is implied that there is a minimum amount of performance acceptable. There is room for much disagreement here. The operational definition one person chooses may be quite unacceptable to another and vice versa.

You may recognize the possibilities listed above as crude performance or behavioral objectives. They are statements of what students might be expected to do as evidence that they "understand fractions." They are also operational definitions because they describe a procedure to use in measuring a variable.

Variable 3: Amount of Evaporation

An investigation is underway to see how the temperature of a liquid affects the "amount of evaporation." Describe at least three ways that "amount of evaporation" could be operationally defined.

_____

_____

_____

_____

X   X   X

Three ways that you may have thought of are:

a. Measure the depth of the liquid. Measure it again twenty-four hours later.
b. Pour a known quantity of liquid into an open container. Measure its volume again three hours later.
c. Mass the container of liquid. Twenty minutes later, mass it again. The difference is the amount of evaporation.

The following is a summary of what you should have learned in this unit.

An operational definition is a definition that describes how to measure a variable. It should state what operation will be performed and what observation will be made. Operational definitions have to be made up. There are usually a variety of ways that one might choose to operationally define a variable. The definition you select depends on your intentions in an investigation.

Now take the self-test for Chapter 14.

Self-test for Chapter 14:

DEFINING VARIABLES OPERATIONALLY.

1. What is an operational definition?
   a. a definition that says how to describe a variable
   b. a definition made up by an expert
   c. a definition that says how to measure a variable
   d. a definition from a reputable dictionary

_____

2. Which of the following could be operational definitions for the variable "knowledge of trees?"
   a. identify at least fifteen different trees on a nature hike
   b. measure the average height of trees
   c. list at least twenty different trees that are native to your state
   d. match pictures of trees with names on a test

_____

3. How are the variables "amount of a liquid" and "solubility of salt" operationally defined in this investigation?

   An investigation is performed to see if the "amount of a liquid" has any effect on the "solubility of salt" in it. (Solubility refers to the capability of dissolving a substance.) Four different amounts of water (50 ml, 100 ml, 150 ml, 200 ml) are placed in identical containers. Salt is added, five grams at a time, to each container. Each is stirred until no salt crystals can be observed in the liquid.

   "amount of liquid" is _____

   _____

   _____

   "solubility of salt" is _____

   _____

   _____

4. Describe three ways that you could operationally define the variable "size of automobile."

   _____

   _____

   _____

   _____

   _____

Check your answers with the Self-test answers.

**SELF-TEST
ANSWERS:
Defining
Variables
Operationally**

1. c
2. A, c, and d could each be an operational definition.
3. "Amount of liquid" is measured in milliliters of water used. "Solubility of salt" is measured by mass of the salt dissolved.
4. Three possibilities are:
   a. Count the number of seats in the car.
   b. Measure the distance between the front and rear bumpers.
   c. Measure the distance between the two front tires.

DESIGNING
INVESTIGATIONS 15

Purpose: In this chapter you will practice designing investigations to test hypotheses. Your skill in designing investigations will be limited only by your imagination. However, this does not mean that your design must be complicated. Quite the contrary, the simpler the design the more likely you will be able to collect usable data.

Objectives: When you have finished this chapter you should be able to:

1. design an investigation to test a given hypothesis.

Approximate time for completion: 30 minutes

An investigation can be defined as the setting up of a planned situation; the situation is planned to yield data about the accuracy of a hypothesis. If the manner in which a variable can be manipulated and the type of response expected is clearly stated in the hypothesis, then much of the work in planning how to collect data has been done. There remains the task of specifying conditions under which the work will be carried out.

Suppose we want to test this hypothesis:

HYPOTHESIS: The greater the surface area of a liquid exposed to the air, the faster evaporation will occur.

The following investigation could be designed.

DESIGN: Pour 100 ml of water at room temperature into each of five aluminum pans that are 5, 6, 7, 8, and 9 cm square. Leave the pans sitting in an open room. After two hours have passed, measure the volume of water remaining in each.

Notice that the design consists of operationally defining the manipulated and responding variables (leaving the liquid in different size open containers and measuring the volume of liquid before and after a specific time) and stating how other variables will be controlled (using the same liquid at the same temperature at the same time in similar containers).

Although most of the investigations used for illustration in this book have used five or six values for the manipulated variable, this number is by no means sacred. The number of points to be recorded depends entirely upon the investigator.

The investigator must decide how many different values of the manipulated variables are appropriate and how they should be selected. For example, if an investigator was interested in the effect of temperature in a plant growing experiment, he would probably not select 10 °C, 12 °C, 14 °C, 16 °C, and 18 °C as the temperatures in which to grow plants. Instead, he would probably select values all the way from boiling to freezing in order to measure temperature effects on plants growing in a wide variety of conditions.

Read the example given below of a hypothesis and the design of an investigation to test it. Then answer the questions about the design.

HYPOTHESIS: The farther a ball drops, the higher it will bounce.
DESIGN OF INVESTIGATION: Release a ball 10 cm above a rigid surface. Record the biggest number that appears under the ball as it rises beside the measuring stick. Repeat this procedure by dropping the ball from heights of 20, 30, 40, and 50 cm.

Questions: a. How was the manipulated variable operationally defined?

_____

b. How was the responding variable operationally defined?

_____

c. What were the variables that were controlled?

_____

d. What values of the manipulated variable were selected for the investigation?

_____

X   X   X

a. The height of a ball above a surface before it was dropped
b. Biggest number that appears under the ball as it rises
c. The same ball is dropped each time on the same surface. The same measuring stick would probably be used although this is not necessary if the sticks are equivalent. The same environmental conditions should prevail throughout the investigation (e.g., amount of wind, temperature, humidity, etc.).
d. 10, 20, 30, 40, and 50 cm.

The four questions you answered above should be considered *each* time you design an investigation. That is, a design should include a description of how both the manipulated and responding variables are operationally defined, what variables will be controlled, and the values of the manipulated variable selected for the investigation. When these four parts are included you have described how the investigation is to be carried out. If you do a good job in writing the design, it should be sufficiently clear that you could hand it to someone else and, without additional instruction, they could carry out the investigation just as you would.

Below is another example of a hypothesis and the design of an investigation to test it. Read the material and answer the questions about the design.

HYPOTHESIS: The greater the concentration of carbon dioxide in the atmosphere, the greater the breathing rate of an animal.

DESIGN: Using a breathing mask, feed air containing .01, .02, .03, and .04% carbon dioxide to different guinea pigs. Count the number of chest movements associated with breathing for five one-minute periods and average for each animal. Use similar sized animals of the same sex and general health.

Questions: a.   How was the manipulated variable operationally defined?

_____

b.   How was the responding variable operationally defined?

_____

c.   What were the variables that were controlled?

_____

d.   What values of the manipulated variable were selected for the investigation?

_____

X   X   X

a.   The percentage of carbon dioxide in the air breathed by the guinea pigs
b.   The average number of chest movements during five one-minute periods
c.   Size, sex, general health, and species of animal. One can also infer that the general environment of the animals would be kept the same throughout the experiment.
d.   .01, .02, .03, and .04% carbon dioxide in the air

Now that you have learned to identify the four parts of a design, try designing an investigation yourself. Design an investigation to test the following hypothesis. Be sure to include how the variables are to be operationally defined, how other variables will be controlled, and what values of the manipulated variable will be used. All of this is usually written up in a brief paragraph.

HYPOTHESIS: The greater the amount of protein in the food of an animal, the more rapid its rate of growth.

DESIGN: _____

_____

_____

_____

_____

_____

_____

X   X   X

Here is just one of several possible designs.

Select a group of five newly weaned guinea pigs of the same size and sex. Feed each animal a basic diet of cereal pellets. Add daily to the diet of one animal 5 gm of protein supplement, add 25 gm daily to another, 50 gm to the third, and 100 gm to the fourth. Record the weight of each animal weekly for five months.

Another hypothesis is given below. Design an investigation to test this hypothesis. Remember to include each of the four parts described previously in your design.

HYPOTHESIS: The greater the concentration of soap in a soap-water mixture, the larger the soap bubble that can be blown.

DESIGN: _____

_____

_____

_____

_____

_____

_____

X   X   X

Here is one possible design.

Dip the bowl of a child's bubble pipe into a mixture of one part liquid soap and twenty parts water. Blow ten bubbles and break each on a clean sheet of white paper. Measure the diameter of the largest splatter. Repeat the procedure for a mixture of one part soap and 15, 10, 5, and 1 part water.

You have now completed the last piece of instruction needed before you design and conduct your own investigation.
Now take the self-test for Chapter 15.

Self-test for Chapter 15:

DESIGNING INVESTIGATIONS

Design an investigation to test each of the following hypotheses:

1. Equal changes in the force needed to stretch a rubberband will cause equal changes in the length of the rubberband.

2. As the amount of water a plant receives each day increases, the amount of plant growth increases.

SELF-TEST ANSWERS: Designing Investigations

These are just two of many possible designs.

1. Suspend the rubberband from some point. Using a hook shaped from a paperclip hang a washer on the rubberband. Measure the distance from where the rubberband is suspended to the paperclip hook. Continue adding washers to the hook one at a time until a total of ten washers are hanging from the rubberband. After each addition, measure the distance between suspension and hook. Using the same rubberband during all measurements will prevent other variables from affecting the outcome.

2. Obtain five bean seedlings each planted in similar pots with the same soil. Place on a window ledge in indirect light. Each day give the first plant 10 ml of water, the second plant 20 ml, the third 30 ml, the fourth 40 ml, and the fifth 50 ml of water. Every second day measure the distance from the soil to the uppermost point on each plant.

EXPERIMENTING 16

Purpose: Experimenting is the activity that puts together all of the science process skills you have learned previously. An experiment may begin as a question. From there the steps in answering the question may include identifying variables, formulating hypotheses, identifying variables to be controlled, making operational definitions, designing an investigation, collecting data, and interpreting data. You will be expected to do all of these in this chapter as you plan and conduct an investigation of your own.

Objective: Following the completion of this chapter, you should be able to:

1. construct a hypothesis, design and conduct an investigation for a problem you have identified or chosen to study.

   Approximate time for completion: One hour (The time may vary significantly depending on the problem you select and your interest in it.)

   Now is the time for you to apply what you have learned in the earlier chapters. Several problems will be suggested from which you may select one to study. The problems are stated as questions that you or your students might ask. You are well equipped to find the answers to them.
   If none of the questions on the following list appeal to you, ask and answer one of your own. Perhaps you are teaching a science unit that has given rise to questions like the ones below. Use one of those questions if you wish.
   These are some of the problems from which you can select. Read them over and then follow the directions on the next page.

1. What affects the amount of time it takes a seed to sprout?
2. What affects the rate at which a person breathes?
3. What affects the amount of salt that can be dissolved in water?
4. What affects the time it takes water to freeze when placed in the freezer section of the refrigerator?
5. What affects the amount of gas produced when vinegar and baking soda are mixed together?
6. What affects how far a rubber band will fly?

7. What affects how far a bath towel can be pulled down across the towel rack before it begins to slide off?
8. What affects the rate at which an object falls through a liquid?
9. What affects the size of a bead of water?
10. What affects the rate at which water flows out of a bottle?

To investigate any of these questions, you should *carry out and report* the following. The report need not be elaborate. One piece of paper should be sufficient to contain all the information in your report. It should include:

1. the statement of the question or problem you are investigating
2. the statement of the hypothesis you are testing
3. a written description of the design of the investigation you will use to test the hypothesis (Remember to describe how the variables are operationally defined, how you will control variables, and what values of the manipulated variable you will use.)
4. reporting the data in a table
5. constructing a graph of the data
6. a statement of the relationship observed between the variables
7. a comparison of your findings with your initial hypothesis to see if the hypothesis was supported or refuted by your investigation

If you run into trouble and would like to see an example of a completed experiment, turn to the next page. Our investigation of "What affects how fast salt dissolves in water?" is given as an example.

When you finish this investigation you will have completed your study of the science process skills in this program. You should seek out frequent opportunities to aid your students in acquiring these skills.

Sample Investigation for Experimenting—16

1. *Problem:* What affects how fast salt dissolves in water?
2. *Hypothesis:* The greater the quantity of salt, the longer it will take to dissolve.
3. *Design:* Differing amounts of salt (6, 12, 18, 24, and 30 grams) will be measured and placed in 250 milliliters of water. The water will be stirred until no more salt crystals are observed and the length of time it takes the salt to disappear will be recorded. The controlled variables are: temperature of all the water, kind of salt used, and the manner of stirring will be the same in all cases.
4. *Data Table:*   5. *Graph:*

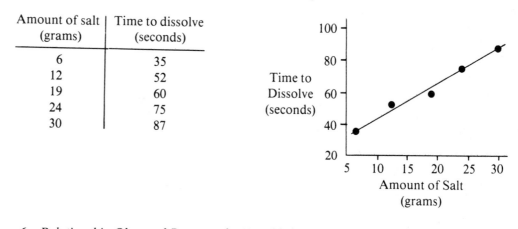

Amount of salt (grams)	Time to dissolve (seconds)
6	35
12	52
19	60
24	75
30	87

6. *Relationship Observed Between the Variables:* The greater the amount of salt added to the water, the longer it took to dissolve.
7. *Findings:* The investigation supported my hypothesis.

Additional Investigations for the Integrated Process Skills

Anything from television commercials to observations of natural phenomena can pose interesting problems that can be studied using the integrated process skills. Following are given some ideas for investigations or projects you may wish to do with your own students.

1. What affects the absorbency of tissues or paper towels?
2. What affects the results of soft drink taste tests? (E.g., would the temperature of the soft drink make a difference?)
3. Is there a relationship between the length of a person's arm and its power?
4. What affects how big a balloon can be inflated using one's lungs?
5. What affects one's reaction time?
6. What affects how quickly one tires?
7. What affects how high a ball will bounce?
8. How much water does a plant need?
9. Can a plant get too much fertilizer?
10. Is there a relationship between the size of a seed and its germination time?
11. What affects the rate at which heat passes through a solid?
12. What affects the size of an inflated balloon?
13. Do some leaves grow faster than others?
14. Does the color of food affect our choice?
15. What affects the boiling point of a liquid?
16. What affects the freezing point of a liquid?

17. What determines the effectiveness of a detergent?
18. What affects the strength of a paper towel?
19. What affects the dissolving rate of an aspirin?
20. What affects the "fastness" of a fabric dye?
21. What affects the strength of concrete?
22. What affects the strength of a single strand of hair?
23. What affects the strength of a thread?
24. What affects the brightness of a burning candle?
25. What affects the length of a service obtained from a flash light cell?
26. What affects the strength of a commercial adhesive?
27. How waterproof are paints?

PART 3

Content, Process, Concepts, and the Nitty Gritty of the Classroom

We as teachers are accountable for the science our students learn. What we do and fail to do in the classroom is important. So, how does a teacher begin to teach science? Begin by teaching the process skills. Teach them the same way you learned them. Grades K-3 should concentrate on the Basic Process Skills, and the higher grades should be learning and using all the process skills. A firm grasp of the skills will enable students to learn the facts and concepts of science by being actively involved with science.

Getting students actively involved means the teacher is selecting or even designing activities for students to do. At the end of this section you'll find a list of activity resource books—valuable tools of the trade. As you discover other good resources, add them to the list. Integrating activities, ideas, and strategies from these resources in your classroom can make the difference between a poor or mediocre science lesson and an effective one.

Activities are one way students get a feel for science and do what scientists do. You should be forewarned, however, that it is possible for a student to do a wonderful job of manipulating materials in an activity and yet not learn the concept for which the activity was designed to teach! This can be very bewildering for the teacher who has been convinced that the hands-on approach is the best way to teach science. When you think about it though, we have all performed an activity of some sort without really understanding what we were supposed to learn. The key here is that it is not the activity that teaches the concept, rather it is the processes the student goes through that lead to the formation of a concept. If the student can manipulate the equipment without applying the process skills, the concept may be missed. How do you know if your students are applying the process skills you have taught them and are learning the desired concepts? Ask! Give students guidance and check their learning throughout the activity by asking questions.

What are the *right* questions to ask to guide students from the facts through the processes to the concepts? First, think about the purpose of the lesson. What do you want them to learn? Just as you would not show a film to a class without first previewing it, do not have students do an activity you have not performed first yourself. While you are doing the activity, formulate and write down the questions you will ask and wish the students to ask when they do the activity. Students have to be taught to ask questions. Praise them for asking good questions; get them interested in their own learning; and let them have fun with science. Get students in the habit of making observations, asking more questions, and making more predictions. End every activity with "What have you learned?"

What follows is an example of a concept, several concepts really, under construction. Follow the model—use it in your classroom—and see how the processes developed in the activities lead students from facts to concepts.

Examine the following activities on plants and seed germination.

GERMINATING SEEDS

For a few cents worth of seeds, you can introduce children to the fascinating realm of plant growth. It is not necessary to provide soil, pots, or windowsill space to have plants growing in your classroom.

Materials Needed:

seeds: corn and bean (vine beans work best)
paper towels
staples
water
plastic sandwich bags: self-locking

Preparation:

Soak the seeds in water overnight to soften the seed coat.

What Do You Observe about Your Seeds?

Have the children make observations about their seeds by examining their shape, color, texture, and size. Have them use their thumbnails to split the seed open to observe the inside.

What Are the Parts of a Seed?

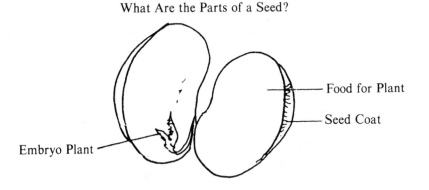

Embryo Plant — Food for Plant — Seed Coat

Children should see the young plant just beginning to develop. The whitish material inside the seed is the stored food that nourishes the new plant. The seed coat protects the seed until the young plant breaks through as germination begins.

What did your students learn from this first activity? (That seeds have three parts: the young plant, stored food, and a seed coat.) Is this true of all seeds? What did they predict?

To test their ideas, have students perform a similar activity with corn seeds. The comparison of the different observations will help students to understand that there are different kinds of plants.

After carefully observing the seeds, students will begin setting up their seed germinators . . .

Here is one kind of germinator your students can make:

1. Fold a paper towel and slip it inside the plastic storage bag to line the bag.
2. Make a row of staples about 4 cm from the bottom of the bag to form a shelf for the seeds to sit on.
3. Place about five seeds inside the bag just above the row of staples.

4. Holding the bag upright, slowly add water to moisten the paper towel and allow a little water to accumulate below the staples. *It will be important to keep the towel moist all during germination.*

5. Close the bag and attach it to the bulletin board where it can be easily observed. If the surface on which you attach the bag is porous, you may wish to cover it first with aluminum foil as moisture may accumulate on the back side of the bag.

Seed Germinator*

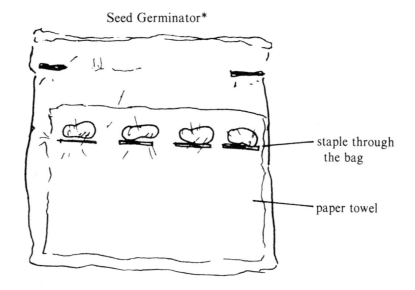

staple through the bag

paper towel

Here is another kind of seed germinator your students can make:

1. Fold a paper towel and use it to line the inside of a clear plastic tumbler.
2. Wad another paper towel and push it into the center of the tumbler to hold the liner in place.
3. Place four or five seeds at equal intervals around the sides of the tumbler between the liner and the tumbler. Be sure the seeds are about 4 cm from the bottom of the tumbler.
4. Moisten the paper towel and *be sure it is kept moist throughout germination.* A lid or plastic wrap on the top of the tumbler will help to keep the liner from drying.

Once your students have set up their germinators, the seeds should begin to sprout in a few days, providing the paper towel liner is kept moist.

*Riley, Joseph and D. K., Sowinski, "Natural Partners: Science and Reading," *Science and Children,* 17:46–47, October, 1979.

What are the parts of the growing young plant?
In what order do you see the parts develop?

Students should first see the root begin to grow and turn downward. Next, the stem will appear and begin growing toward the source of light. Then leaves will appear and develop.

**What Do the
Plant Parts Do?**

Start simple . . .
Begin by sacrificing three plants. Have students use ones they have grown if you wish . . .

Take one of the plants and cut off all its leaves. Continue watering and caring for the plant as you normally would. What happens to the plant after several days? (The plant will eventually die—the leaves must perform some function necessary for survival.)

Take another of the plants and cut away its stem. You'll first notice the leaves fall away. (The stem supports the leaves in light and air.) Also observe that the roots and leaves are no longer connected. (The stem is a pathway between the roots and leaves.) What happens to the plant without its stem?

Cut off the roots of the third plant. Try to stand the plant up. (The roots serve to anchor the plant and hold it up.) Continue to observe the plant for several days. What happens to the plant? (The plant will eventually die—the roots must perform a function necessary for the plant to survive.)

Let's Learn More

Have some students place their plants in a place where they will receive no sunlight. (Even if the plants are well watered, eventually they will die. This illustrates the fact that plants need sunlight in order to grow.)

Have the students observe a leaf closely using a magnifying glass. They should see tiny pores on the underside of the leaf. Have the students plug the pores of a leaf of a plant with a layer of vasoline. What happens to the leaf after a few days? (The pores are tiny openings that allow for the exchange of oxygen and carbon dioxide in the leaf.) The leaves of the plant are where food making takes place. All green leaves contain chlorophyll, the substance necessary for food making. Leaves use water and dissolved minerals, carbon dioxide from the air, and light from the sun to make food for the plant.

The water and dissolved materials needed by the leaves for food making are absorbed by the roots and carried upwards by the stem. To illustrate the transport of fluids through a stem, place a stalk of celery in a glass of colored water. Red or blue coloring works best. Observe the celery stalk, or stem, for a few hours. Students should see the colored water being drawn up through the stem.

Cut or break the celery
stalk just before placing
it in the coloring.

Look again at the roots of a young plant, this time with a magnifying glass. Students should see tiny hairs near the tip of the roots (root hairs). They may at first look like a fuzzy growth. The root hairs add greatly to the amount of root surface in contact with the soil so that more water with dissolved minerals can enter the roots. Carefully remove the root hairs of one seedling and compare that seedling's growth with that of a seedling with root hairs. Be sure to keep both seedlings moist and continue to observe them for several days.

What have they learned from this?

1. Some seeds have three parts; some do not.
2. There are differences in plant seeds.
3. Plants have roots, stems, leaves, (and flowers and seeds, given luck).
4. Plant parts differ.
5. Plants need certain things in order to live.
6. Leaves are where food making takes place; stems support the plant and transport water and minerals to the leaves; roots absorb water and minerals from the soil.
7. Each plant part performs a function important to the life of the plant.

There's More to Learn About Plants

Keep it going. . . . You'll find many more ideas in the activity sourcebooks. Here are some more ideas to investigate about plants;

1. Do plants bend toward the light or away from it? How can you find out? How does a plant bend?
2. Do roots always grow down and stems always grow up? What happens if you turn the plant upside down for a while?
3. Choose a plant that grows well in an environment very different from the one in which you live. What is it about that plant that allows it to survive there?
4. Think about this one:

   Ten years ago a tree was twenty feet high, one foot in diameter, and its first branch was six feet above the ground. Now that same tree is forty feet high and twenty inches in diameter. Now how far from the ground is that first limb?

Activity Sourcebooks

Abruscato, Joseph, *Teaching Children Science,* Prentice-Hall, Inc., Englewood Cliffs, NJ, 1982.

Cain, Sandra E. and Evans, Jack M., *Sciencing,* 2nd edition, Charles Merrill, A Bell and Howell Company, 1984.

DeVito, Alfred, and Gerald H. Krockover, *Creative Sciencing: A Practical Approach,* Boston: Little, Brown and Company, 1980.

Esler, William K. *Teaching Elementary Science,* 2nd edition, Wadsworth Publishing Company, Inc., 1977.

Gega, Peter C., *Science in Elementary Education,* 4th edition, John Wiley and Sons, Inc., 1982.

George, Kenneth D., Dietz, Marueen A., Abraham, Eugene C., Nelson, Miles A., *Elementary School Science—Why and How,* D. C. Heath and Company, 1974.

Munson, Howard R., *Science with Simple Things,* Fearon Publishers, Inc., 1972.

Nelson, Leslie W., and Lorbeer, George C., *Science Activities for Elementary Children,* 8th edition, Wm. C. Brown Publishers, 1984.

Schmidt, Victor E. and Rockcastle, Verne N., *Teaching Science with Everyday Things,* 2nd edition, McGraw-Hill, Inc., 1982.

Strongin, Herb, *Science on a Shoestring,* Addison-Wesley Publishing Company, 1976.

Victor, Edward, *Science for the Elementary School,* 4th edition, Macmillan Publishing Company, Inc., 1980.

Wolfinger, Donna M., *Teaching Science in the Elementary School: Content, Process, and Attitude,* Little, Brown and Company, 1984.

APPENDIX

Materials and Equipment for Learning Science Process Skills

EQUIPMENT AND MATERIALS

The materials listed below are needed to do the exercises in this book. The materials are simple and inexpensive. Many of the materials can be found at home or purchased locally. The most expensive item on the list is a double-pan balance and masses. A functional one could be constructed by students. No materials are listed for Chapter 16 because the materials depend on which problem is chosen to be investigated.

Item	Amount	Used in Chapters
plant	1	1
sugar cube	1 box	1
birthday candle	1 box	1
clay	25 grams	1
matches	1 book	1
chewing gum	1 stick/student	1
balance and masses	1	1, 4
meter stick	1	1, 4, 5
scissors	1	3
centicubes	20	4
baby food jars	5	4, 7, 11
large sinkers	10	4, 5
liter container	1	4, 7
assorted containers	4	4, 7
graduated cylinder 50 ml or larger	1	4, 11
marbles	5	4
washers	1	4
numbered buttons labeled a) Multiple Properties b) Multi-stage Classification (#1–6)	2 assortments	2
cereal box information panels	1 assortment	2

buttons or beads	25 red	5
	10 blue	
	10 green	
	5 white	
sugar	—	11
ice cubes	—	4
thermometer (0-120°C)	1	4, 7, 11
100 ml pyrex beakers	4	11
toothpick	1 box	4
string	2 meters	5, 11
circuit tester (battery, three wires, and bulb)	1	6
inference board	1	6
mystery box	1	6
spring balance	1	11
alcohol burner	1	11
calcium chloride	500 grams	7
spoon (plastic)	1	7, 11
burner support	1	11
timer	1	11
wooden block	1	11
rubber tubing	4 tubes (about 50 cm long, each with a different diameter)	11

Notes:
1. With equipment such as balances, graduated cylinders and plants, it would be better to have two to four of each for larger classes.
2. The inference board would have to be constructed for the wiring pattern shown in Chapter 6.
3. The optional activity in Chapter 5 requires a glass jar and enough particles (marbles, peas, rice, etc.) to fill the jar.

NOTES

NOTES

NOTES

NOTES

NOTES